REDISTRIBUTIVE MODELING:

KNOW YOUR OPTIONS

Ronald M. Karren

REDISTRIBUTIVE MODELING: KNOW YOUR OPTIONS

Version 7.6

ISBN 978-1-62407-683-1

Ronald M. Karren
ron@americanfinancialplanner.com
American Financial Planner, Inc.
P.O. Box 1286
Pleasant Grove, UT 84062
800-614-1550

INTRODUCTION

What you are about to discover are tangible, viable solutions to a problematic phenomenon that has plagued human society from the beginning of recorded history. As a matter of fact, this same phenomenon is played out innumerable times daily throughout the animal kingdom. It can be observed in just about any wildlife documentary wherein animals of prey such as the female cheetah (with two cubs in the den), meticulously calculates and strategizes the landing of their next meal. Upon landing that meal, it is all too often taken by a lion or a pack of hyenas—before the cheetah can even recoup the *investment of energy*. Does anyone get that *warm and fuzzy feeling* when they witness the worker/producer being robbed of her production?

This same phenomenon is also seen in the less-aggressive species; those animals that put forth the time and efforts to gather and store their food source against the oncoming season of scarcity, only to have others come along and raid the cache. It is played out in our backyards where a squirrel's cache of acorns is raided by a neighboring squirrel, while the producing squirrel is out doing the work. In the mind of most people, this phenomenon inevitably invokes a feeling of unfairness, regardless of the person's political persuasion.

In the human realm, history exposes equally (if not more) barbaric behaviors. Marauding Goths, Huns, Vikings, and other aggressive societies would raid and pillage neighboring towns and tribes to take what they had. As more "civilized" governments began to form, the phenomenon did not change much; Egyptian pharaohs, Roman emperors, and Chinese dynasties conquered entire regions or countries to *confiscate* what those populations had produced. These evolved into power-concentration centers such as monarchies and even power-wielding religions. And, in short, the producing masses eventually revolted.

Today, it appears the pendulum has swung dramatically in favor of the masses. And, historically, imbalanced pendulum swinging seldom produces positive outcomes. The *new* confiscation measures carry a kinder, gentler label: *Redistribution of Wealth*, which concept connotes different things to different geo-political groups. The ways and means to bring the redistribution about is through fiscal/political policy, taxation, or other social-justice measures. However, the purpose of this book is not to delve into the *redistribution-of-wealth* debate. The purpose of this book is to expose you to the reality that there are many more options available in the *redistributive* realm; namely, the leveling of the playing field via the *redistribution of equal opportunity*. In that our economy is so vast and continually evolving, there are several *redistributive models* that are much more attractive than the narrowly-defined tenets of today's coined concept *Redistribution of Wealth*. In these new *redistributive models*, all households in all classes benefit, as does the establishment. What is more exciting is that there are numerous options available within each *redistributive model*.

The *redistributive models* that you are about to discover are structured in such a manner that the *redistribution of revenue* comes about naturally through the behavioral changes of the consumer—*i.e.* how they act, react, and transact in the current system. The redirected flow of funds in *these* models takes place before funds are earned by and/or distributed to individuals (in other words: while it is still considered *revenue*, and before it is considered *salary* or *wealth*). This alleviates the battles that arise when you *take from the haves and give to the have-nots* (after the productive efforts have been put forth). Wherein changes in the older (archaic) systems were brought about by the *dollar vote* concept, these models are more dynamic and more powerful, where dramatic changes are brought about by *behavioral vote*.

Five notable *redistributive models* can be found in the *mortgage finance, retirement finance, healthcare, employee benefits,* and *consumable-goods* industries. Through the first decade of research & development and in market testing, the author (and his clientele living these concepts) have created an average of $164,000 in mortgage-interest savings, $100,000 in retirement account production (above the *government- qualified*, *pre-tax* structure), and $60,000 savings in healthcare premiums and costs; over this initial 10-year period. The average home-owning American can save $300,000 over a 10-year period within the first four models. Even individuals, who are neither in a home nor contributing to a retirement plan, can now arrive at that financial disposition much more quickly by learning about these *redistributive* models and following the respective principles of each.

The *redistributive models* are easy to learn and implement. It requires that you know your options—Key Word: KNOW. This requires education on your part. And, as the author has maintained and practiced throughout this 10-year financial expedition, the educational seminars and webinars have always been (and remain) free of charge; however, even free education requires effort.

ACKNOWLEDGMENTS

This work really belongs to myriad individuals with whom I have sat, supped, configured and conversed on seemingly endless financial topics. Hence, both this book and the collection of financial concepts have come together, as a puzzle, over time.

As you will find, these products correlate almost chronologically in relation to the life stages of the typical American; namely credit (and credit-related issues), mortgages and mortgage acceleration, asset protection, tax strategies (which come and go dynamically with the changing political landscape), and lastly, retirement strategies, or more precisely, tax-free/no-market loss retirement strategies.

Being fiscally conservative, these financial concepts had notable impact on me when I first came across them. After their discovery, I immediately took the new concepts into various test-marketing scenarios, going head-to-head with CPAs and various financial planners. If I could win them over *and* the concepts were relatively conservative, then I could feasibly project a successful rate of penetration and application in the market place.

Throughout this work, I will share actual stories of how I discovered and applied these financial formulations personally, as well as to the clientele base—as each application varied with each client's unique financial construct.

Lastly, this book is dedicated to my clients who, through their trust and the process of working through their initial skepticism over these past ten years, have allowed me to move these concepts forward (*i.e.* to prove the formulations sufficiently to take them to the masses).

Thanks to each of you!

Table of Contents

Table of Contents

PART I: MORTGAGE FINANCE MODELING

Chapter 1: Thriving in Evolving Economies

To understand *where we are* as a nation *financially* we must acquire a basic understanding of *where we have been* as a nation *financially.* Why? Because despite the evolution of our economies (four of them in the past 70 years), we are still using the financial devices that were put in place over 100 years ago.

The Gold Standard

The *gold standard* was a system that arose out of a nearly 4000 year-old concept of creating coinage out of precious metals (typically gold or silver). In these early systems the value of the coin was simply determined by its weight.

In the mid-1700s, there was a trade imbalance between China and Europe causing a shortage of these precious metals in Europe. From this crisis grew the concept of issuing *bank notes* or *stock notes* (a paper-based monetary system) that required the issuer (normally a bank) to provide gold to the holder of the that note upon demand.

The United States used the gold standard until 1933. In 1934, Congress passed *The Gold Reserve Act*, which was in force until 1944 when the U.S. entered the *Bretton Woods International Monetary System*. This system was established among the Allied Nations engaged in World War II to expand trade through borrowing and lending between the allies. This system was still based on a *gold-on-demand* system, but used paper notes as currency.

The Fiat Economy

By 1971, the U.S. abandoned the Bretton Woods system and went to a strictly paper currency, which was no longer backed by gold, but simply backed by the U.S. government's "word" or "promise" to back the money they print (chalk this one up to Nixon and the conservative right). Hence, by "authority" or by authoritative *fiat*, the government can simply say, "our dollar is worth X amount, and we will back our own dollars with our word".

In reality however, instead of backing up those dollars, we normally just print more, and write an I.O.U. Yes, there are many downsides to simply printing more money, like the devaluation of the dollar compared to other foreign currencies, inflation, etc. As the dollar becomes worth less, merchants demand more dollars for their merchandise thereby creating a downward spiral.

The fiat economy opened the door to *paper-based economy*, wherein the printed paper was no longer a *payable note* or a *promissory note*. It was simply a piece of paper that held a *decreed value*. With web applications, electronic depositing, online banking, the universality of credit cards, and the implementation of paperless statements, we have now evolved well into a digitally- or electronically-based fiat economy with all its pros and cons—more cons than pros as far as fraud, money laundering, etc. as there are fewer systemic checks and balances.

The fiat economy is nearly 40 years old as we officially exited the Bretton Woods system in 1971. If the *checking account* and the *savings account* were established back when we were on the gold standard and employed throughout the entire Bretton Woods system (1944 to 1971), then why would we still be using these archaic, out-dated financial vehicles that do nothing for us, except continue to keep us in debt? It is comparable to e-mail vs. postal mail. And, since *time* is a key factor in *interest*, why not move to vehicles better suited for *the instantaneous electronic fiat economy*?

Moreover, if we have evolved to the *fiat currency* (and hence, a *fiat economy* where that currency is only as good as the next quarterly "authoritative decree" from the Secretary of the Treasury), then why are we still operating in *unproductive cash accounts* rather than *credit or debit accounts*?

Now that you have the basic historical overview, let me put it in everyday terms: If you bring in a $5,000 paycheck and deposit that into the typical U.S. checking account, how much do you make on that money? In most cases: Nothing.

How long does that $5,000 paycheck actually sit in the checking account before you have to pay your mortgage or other living expenses? Five days? Ten days? Twenty days?

Each day that $5,000 is sitting in the typical checking account, you make nothing on that money, while the bank either invests it making anywhere from 10% to 30% or more; or, it applies those funds against the line(s) of credit that it uses to fund its investments. In reality, they are taking your money and putting it against their debts, thereby reducing their *daily calculated interest*.

What if that $5,000 paycheck, instead of sitting in the checking account benefitting the bank, could sit against YOUR debt for those ten to twenty days? If you had $5,000 that could sit against YOUR $200,000 mortgage for twenty days out of the month, *and* the daily calculated interest of that first mortgage was then based on a $195,000 balance for those twenty days, and then went back up to $200,000 for the following ten days (because you needed the money to pay for living expenses), how much savings in Daily Calculated Interest would that create over time?

This, in its simplest form, is a daily banking behavior in the Australian banking system, and the basis for the modern *mortgage acceleration concept*.

Here in the U.S. during the first 8 years of a $195,000 mortgage, on the first payment we are assessed daily calculated interest on $194,900 because we will typically pay down only $100 in principal. On each month of your mortgage, would you rather be assessed daily calculated interest on $194,900 for 30 days of the month, or on $190,000 for 20 days, and the $191,000 on the ensuing 3 days, and then on $193,000 from day 24 to day 29, and then 194,500 on days 30 and 31? Then when the new paycheck comes in, you are then assessed daily calculated interest on $189,500 for the next 20 days. The alternative to Month 2 in this scenario is to be assessed daily calculated interest on $194, 800 for 30 days, only gaining $100 each month.

Now, those of you who work in the banking industry will say, "Yes, but this type of account does not exist" (*i.e.* one in which you can put your entire paycheck against your mortgage, and then pull it right back out again ten or twenty days later to pay your bills).

Well, there was an account on U.S. soil that did exactly that, but unfortunately the small company offering that account went out of business with the last economic downturn. However, if it did exist, you still wouldn't want to use it as structured for the U.S. It is simply too risky putting your entire mortgage on an interest-only loan with a variable interest rate.

By reconfiguring the use of everyday over-the-counter banking products already in place within the U.S. banking system, we can easily outperform any Australian-type mortgage product simply by modifying our daily banking and finance behaviors.

Before addressing these behaviors, my objective with each of my clients is to transition them from what I call the *cash economy vehicles* to the *fiat economy vehicles*, or from *cash accounts* to *debt accounts.* Though this may sound sketchy, think of it as *fighting fire with fire*, using good debt to fight bad debt.

If you wish to cut your mortgage and consumer-debt interest to one-third (or less), you will need to fight those debts with more effective debt vehicles, e.g. vehicles that are better suited for this *instantaneous* and *electronic* fiat economy.

Old Vehicles vs. New Vehicles

The evolution of our currencies and economies (and to a limited extent the banking products) has resulted in a financial structure where our financial accounts are separated both physically and psychologically. I have clients with a mortgage, a savings account, a checking account, and sometimes up to twenty or more revolving credit accounts and loans resulting in a monthly money shuffle in twenty five different directions.

Because the mortgage itself is a 30-year black hole that we cannot even fathom paying off (which in itself creates a flawed lifestyle), we allocate our discretionary income to "financing things". The thinking in this country is such that the home will not be paid off until our children become parents themselves (30 years); therefore, no priority is given to paying off the home. Hence, we Americans take the position that we want various toys to enjoy with our kids while they are still young (*i.e.* boats, ATVs, campers, etc.). In essence, our lifestyle is determined by how much we can *finance*.

If we have $1,000/month of *discretionary income* (money left over after the mortgage, living expenses and other debts are paid), we like to think that this is money we can use to go spend or with which we can finance things. With $1,000 of discretionary income, we can now afford a second car for $400/month and two ATVs at $250/month, a $50/month gym membership, and so on and so forth until we are living in a *hand-to-mouth* environment where every cent is spent before it comes in. Any incentive for paying off the mortgage is removed, or better stated, *any possibility* of paying down the mortgage in an accelerated manner is now gone.

Moreover, we have financial advisors and even CPAs and accountants warning, "If you pay your home off, you will lose your mortgage interest tax write-off. Therefore, don't engage in mortgage acceleration." Why would anyone want to *have to pay* the bank $1,000/month in interest so that he could receive a $300/month tax write-off (in the 30% tax bracket or $200 in the 20% tax bracket)? Pay off your mortgage, pay your $300 tax bill, and pocket that remaining $700 that is currently going to the bank in the form of interest. Or, go find a more efficient tax shelter.

> [Side Bar: There is something much better than a tax write-off: Not having to pay the bill at all.]

Within the old financial structure and conditioning, if we have money left over at the end of the month, we take the leftover funds from the checking account and transfer them into a savings account. If we were able to continue on this pattern with surplus funds every month, the ambitious amongst us would typically begin to put extra principal against the mortgage—an extremely dangerous proposition in our current financial structure without having a *buffer account* in place.

If you were one of those unfortunate individuals who paid large sums of money against your mortgage, and then subsequently lost your job or were laid up with an injury, chances are you became a victim of the robust, thriving industry known as *Foreclosure*.

Putting large sums of money against your mortgage is extremely dangerous if you don't have that safety net in place in the case of job loss or injury. This *buffer account* created by your home equity is a terrific safety net. In a dire financial strait, don't think that you can just run to a loan officer and refinance the house in order to get your money back out. Remember, you just lost your job, and therefore, you can't qualify for a refinance. If you were injured and can't work, you won't have the check stubs to prove the necessary income to qualify. Additionally, refinancing is an expensive way to get those extra payments back out of your home should you need that money.

The new debt account, any *line of credit* (such as a Home Equity Line of Credit—HELOC) can serve as a *buffer* account, allowing us to accomplish a safe, secure, and conservative approach to mortgage acceleration. As you pay down the first mortgage, you should expand (or increase) the HELOC so that you have access to the money you have put against the first mortgage in case you need it. This can be done every year or every other year depending on how much mortgage reduction you have created, and depending on your financial institution's policies.

Transitioning into the *Old* New Economy

As stated earlier, the current economy was put in motion in 1971 when our currency became a *fiat currency.* Hence, this *new fiat economy* is really quite *old*, nearly forty years old at the printing of this book. Yet, we are still living and utilizing archaic financial vehicles that prohibit *your* money from working for *you*. Keeping your money in archaic cash accounts (like checking and savings accounts) *only* inures to the bank's benefit.

Banks will take your money, invest it, and make 10 to 30 percent on that money, paying you 1% to 3% if it is in a CD, 1% (or less) if it is in a savings account, and 0% if your money is in a checking account. So what happens when the bank invests your money in bad investments and loses? They go out of business, some go to jail, and you may or may not get your money back.

> [Sidebar: This scenario is the basic description of the Savings & Loan meltdown in the 1980's. Bankers speculated in oil and gas and lost big money, requiring a taxpayer bailout.]

In transitioning into the new economy with the new, more efficient concepts, *you* use *your* money to *your* benefit (to accelerate the elimination of consumer debt first, and then to eliminate the mortgage).

Additionally, the mortgage acceleration program speedily creates a larger and larger safety net or nest egg by buying down the mortgage and continually expanding the HELOC (or increasing the amount of money that is available to you in the HELOC).

The first step is to replace your checking account with what I call a *buffer account*. The account of choice is a Home Equity Line of Credit (HELOC). Though you will continue to use the checking account on a very limited basis, the majority of your financial activity will take place within the HELOC.

> [Side Bar: Since Black October 2008, I have discovered other Lines of Credit that are more easily obtained and that work just as efficiently. Therefore, just because I will be referring to a HELOC throughout this text as the "buffer account," keep in mind that for the most part, any line of credit will work with this system.]

If you cannot qualify for a HELOC, you may employ the use of a Personal Line of Credit (P-LOC) or a Business Line of Credit (B-LOC). I have even temporarily configured a buffer account with a credit card. Typically, HELOCs are the most convenient, and we will eventually want to evolve to a HELOC when there is adequate equity in the property to obtain a HELOC.

Just as important as the *buffer account* is the concept of *online banking.* Online banking allows you to easily and efficiently transfer your funds from one account to another. Because we are charged *daily calculated interest*, the ability to move funds from these accounts at any given time becomes crucial.

> [Side Bar: In case you are worried, this system is not labor intensive.]

Though, in the new system, the checking account has a lesser role, we do maintain a checking account because HELOC's and PLOC's don't contain *routing numbers* (unless a special checking account is integrated with them). So as long as *routing numbers* are the backbone of the American banking system, enabling such activities as the wiring of funds and electronic deposits, we must hold on to the checking account. The checking account, then, has two uses: To facilitate *electronic deposits* from your employer, and to facilitate payments to a creditor who does not accept credit cards for payment such as a gardener, piano teacher, or maid.

I further recommend that you employ the use of a credit card on which to put as many of your monthly living expenses as possible. Why? It enables you to leverage money over time each month with no interest. It amounts to interest-free living enabling you to keep your line of credit as low as possible throughout the month, which saves daily calculated interest.

Example:
Let's say that a bank just gave us a HELOC with a credit line of $100,000. Keep in mind we are only charged interest on the amount of money we pull from that HELOC. You qualified for $100,000, but you only pulled $10,000 out and put it against your first mortgage. With this transfer from the HELOC to the first mortgage, the balance on our first mortgage was reduced from $150,000 down to $140,000.

Now in the first mortgage, we are charged daily calculated interest each and every day from that point forth on $140,000 rather than on $150,000.

Returning to the HELOC that now has a $10,000 balance, let's say we have a $5,000 paycheck that came in. We go online that day, and transfer the $5,000 paycheck from the checking account to the HELOC, reducing that balance from $10,000 to $5,000. Hence, from that day forth, we are charged daily calculated Interest on $5,000 rather than on $10,000.

By placing as many of our expenses as possible on the credit card, our entire paycheck is able to sit against the HELOC balance, which was originally $10,000. When it is time to pay the living expenses amassed on the credit card (timely enough so that there are no interest charges from the credit card company), the balance in the HELOC rises back up to $8,000 (given that this family has living expenses of $3,000/month).

However shortly thereafter, we have another paycheck of $5,000 coming in, which is transferred into the HELOC, reducing our HELOC balance down to $3,000.

Bottom line: In this new system your paycheck is able to sit against your debt for ten, twenty, or even twenty-five days, reducing your daily calculated interest for one-third to two-thirds of the month. In this manner, you are also able to reduce the interest you would normally pay on the typical mortgage by 50% to 75%. In essence this system creates the equivalent of *reverse compound interest* inuring to *your* benefit. The enormous cogs of the *Redistribution of Wealth* machine are starting to turn.

The accuracy of the entire system is calculated on your income and expenses and the system requires that you have a positive cash flow. However, don't be discouraged. In most cases, for consumers with no positive cash flow and much consumer debt, a few simple consolidation plays are normally sufficient to create a positive cash flow scenario, enabling the system to work for you.

There are a few companies whose websites contain math engines that will tell you right off the bat whether or not they can help you, some more reliable and/or accurate than others. However, if you get the thumbs down from any other mortgage acceleration provider stating your cash flow is insufficient, contact me. Chances are my staff can configure something that will work in your situation.

We certainly can't end the subject of transitioning accounts until we address the conservatively sanctioned *Savings Account.* I have had a wide variety of clients with $20,000 to $40,000 in their savings accounts and, generally speaking, this is a waste of both *time* and *money*.

Example:
I have a client with a home valued at $280,000. However, his mortgage balance was only $110,000. The interest rate on

his mortgage was 6.75% and he had $40,000 sitting in his savings account earning the typical 1%.

We obtained a HELOC of $130,000. We then took his $40,000 savings and put it against his first mortgage of $110,000 reducing it instantaneously to $70,000. His principal-to-interest ratio (of his payments) in the first mortgage was drastically improved, gaining much *more principal* with each payment with much *less of each payment* going toward interest.

By transferring $40,000 out of the savings account that was earning him 1% and putting it against his mortgage where he was paying 6.75% interest, he instantaneously gained 5.75% on that $40,000 from that point forward.

We then returned to the bank to extend his line of credit from $130,000 to $170,000 (the original $130,000 HELOC plus the $40,000 of additional equity that we created by moving the savings account against the mortgage).

Some of my clients, still operating under the stigma of the Great Depression, balk at transferring funds from a savings account to the mortgage. I recently had a client with $50,000 in her savings account who only wished to move half of it over against the mortgage—despite the fact that she had roughly $500,000 available through the HELOC.

Being conservative and playing the role of educator, I never push my clients. I simply provide the math, the possible scenarios, and then allow them to choose the path that works best for them. I am confident, however, that this client will move the remaining $25,000 in time. Even in this recessive economy, she still has a large safety net in the HELOC, even if the bank decides to lower her credit limit. Depending on the client's financial disposition, it is a wise idea for an individual to have cash on hand in a recessive period.

Many consumers find security or peace of mind having their money in a banking institution with, “Well, at least the FDIC insures $250,000 of my money”.

Correction: Your $250,000 will be worth less than 10 cents on the dollar if more than 1.25% of the banks fail. See Chapter 7 for details on the actual value of FDIC protection.

Back to the HELOC: It is important to know that traditionally the more money you qualify for in a HELOC, the better the interest rate the bank will extend to you. This lower interest rate provides the incentive for borrowers to use that HELOC. Only by using the HELOC does the bank make money. The more money you use, the more interest they make.

Lastly, living in a debt account such as a HELOC certainly doesn’t seem to be a “conservative” approach to finance. But in reality, it is the most conservative thing one can do as it enables consumers to pay off their mortgages in an average of less than 9 years. It doesn’t get any more conservative than that.

Within the new system, we consolidate consumer debt into a much more efficient debt vehicle, transition out of the *cash accounts* and into *debt accounts*, and then begin leveraging good debt (HELOC) against bad debt (consumer accounts) and then against long-term debt (the mortgage).

Foreclosure

For those of you who may be new to mortgages or purchasing a home, the term *foreclosure* simply means *the bank takes possession of your home* (normally selling it at a foreclosure sale or auction). Foreclosure happens because you stopped paying the bank for the money they loaned you to purchase your home. Because you stopped paying them, the bank can now have the sheriff evict you from your home after a period of 60, 90, or 120 days, depending on the state in which you live, and depending on the fine print within your mortgage contract.

Though you may not know anyone first hand who has experienced *foreclosure*, it is a thriving industry. People fall into financial difficulties and eventually lose their homes.

Many of you in the more experienced generation will think in this manner: *I have been doing business with this bank for so long, and I have always made my payments on time* (*and often early*), and *my home is nearly paid off. Therefore, if I get behind on my payments, my bank will work with me.* This is a false notion. For banks, foreclosure is not an *emotional* decision: It is a *financial* decision.

If you have substantial equity in your home, you are a prime target for foreclosure. Banks make money foreclosing on you because they can sell your home cheaply, very quickly, and still make good money on the sale.

Conversely, if you have very little equity in the home (some call it *being mortgaged to the hilt*), the bank does not want to foreclose on you, as it would cost them money to take it from you and then try to sell it. If your home is valued at $350,000 and your mortgage balance is $345,000, banks don't want to foreclose on your home. There is no money in it for them.

Those of the problem-solving ilk might think in this manner: *If I have substantial equity in my home, and then I lose my job, then I will simply go refinance my home and pull cash out to hold me over until I get another job.*

If you lost your job, don't think you are going to be able to refinance your home to get cash out, or even qualify for a HELOC. You need a job with a current pay stub to qualify for either of these solutions. Hence, if you cannot quickly sell the home, you will most likely fall victim to foreclosure, losing all of the equity you have built over the years.

Now the big question: Why do I want to pay my mortgage down if it puts me at higher risk of foreclosure?

Answer: For several reasons: 1) The cost of your mortgage, in terms of the interest you will pay on that mortgage, will keep you in debt for 30 years or longer, usually paying one-and-a-half to two times the actual cost of the home. 2) The American dream isn't to have a *mortgage*, but rather, to own a *home* on a parcel of *land* that is completely paid for, and 3) If you have a mortgage, you are on what I call, the *defensive* side of finance, rather than on the *offensive* side. (This concept is explained under the section entitled, *Becoming Your Own Bank.*)

In this new financial system, foreclosure becomes a thing of the past. This new system creates a phenomenal *safety net* or as our parents have often called it, *a rainy-day fund,* which can save you from foreclosure. Frankly, in this new system we now have a rainy-day fund on steroids—the HELOC.

Resolution

Let's revisit the example of my client with the $280,000 home. Remember, his mortgage balance is only $110,000, leaving him $170,000 in equity (the portion he owns). Such substantial equity makes him a prime target for foreclosure and also lawsuits. Why? Because cash assets and home equity are the first targets in the legal realm.

However, if you have a Home Equity Line of Credit for the $170,000, that money is accessible with the swipe of a card or the writing of a check. If you are laid off from work or injured, you won't have to qualify for a HELOC. It's already in place. You qualified for it *before* the incident.

Hence, you simply write checks for your mortgage and/or living expenses from the HELOC, allowing you to clearly and calmly think and plan out what steps need to be taken to get you back on your feet again. You are removed from the stress of a quick sale of your home.

For most of my clients, the $170,000 protection from the HELOC would provide ample time to find new work, heal from injury, or even put the home on the market and allow sufficient time for it to sell, removed from the stress and duress of foreclosure . The HELOC can be the ultimate rainy-day fund, or safety net.

This is the point where many of my clients quip: *But if I take this money out, I have to pay it back with interest.*

Even so, this is a far better option than losing your home through foreclosure and being paid pennies on the dollar because it was sold at a bank auction. If you were in this position with a HELOC in place, you could actually live on $160,000 of that equity, which would give you sufficient time to put the house on the market and sell it for the right price. You sell the home for the value of $280,000, paying off your $110,000 first mortgage, as well as paying off the $60,000 portion of the Home Equity Line of Credit you used for living expenses for 18 months (or so). You would then be left with your $100,000 of equity, minus realtor fees and other sales costs. This is a much better proposition than attempting to pay down your mortgage without the HELOC (or a *buffer account*) in place.

This, however, is a *defensive* outlook or use of this account. There are much more productive and progressive uses and benefits, which I detail in Chapter 4.

Bottom line: You don't want to attempt paying your mortgage down without a buffer account in place. If your home is already paid off (or close to it), obtain a HELOC for as much as the lending institution will offer you as soon as possible. You don't need to use the money. You just want the ability to access this equity at the drop of a hat should you need to get to it. What you don't use, you don't pay for.

With that said, if you are prone to spend money when you have a line of credit, don't go down this road unless you have specific scheduling (or assistance) on how to manage it. You don't want to establish a HELOC, run up the account, and then have two mortgages to pay off. If you are wise, this account can be a tremendous springboard to transition you from the *defensive* side of finance to the *offensive* side. There are many financial strategies for this demographic of homeowners.

In the post-back-to-back recession era of 2001 and 2008, many banks have locked their HELOCs transitioning them into fixed loans because home values have dropped below the balance of the mortgage and HELOC combined. If this happens (or has already happened), we will simply treat the HELOC as another debt, and use either a personal line of credit or even a secured line of credit as the mortgage-accelerator account.

One more note on HELOCs before moving on: Obtaining a HELOC can be about as fun as having a root canal. If you are looking to obtain a HELOC, you can usually obtain one *at no cost* at your local bank or credit union. If the bank is going to charge you for an appraisal or other fees, contact my staff and they can (in most cases) inform you of where and how to obtain the best HELOC or other line of credit at a local bank or credit union.

If you obtain a HELOC on your own, be sure to get it from an institution that offers full-service online banking, enabling you to transfer funds between the HELOC and the checking account within their online banking structure. Be sure to ask about the fees for transferring funds from the HELOC to the checking account and visa versa. There should be no fees unless the bank makes the transfers for you automatically.

Chapter 2: Discovering the Concepts

Because the subject of my background and qualifications are usually the third or fourth most frequently asked questions by prospective clients, I feel it is important to expound on them.

The concepts, herein, appear to go against most everything we have heard throughout our adult/financial lives, they tend to spawn an above-average flurry of skepticism. Because of this skepticism, I'm quite sure my degree in Political Science and International Relations won't necessarily sway you to my side of the financial spectrum. Therefore, I am obliged to lay out the landscape of the inception, development, as well as the perfecting process of these formulations and concepts. It has been an amazing (and sometimes frustrating) journey.

Moreover, given my background, I doubt that anyone (including myself) would have thought I would be on the cutting edge of finance, helping to bring about change in five of the largest industries in the world: *Mortgage, Mortgage Finance, Retirement, Insurance, and Employee Benefits*, all of which affect other interrelated and interdependent industries. The adherence to these concepts by the masses would bolster the middle class while improving the finances of the lower by creating a massive redistribution of wealth through the free-market system (as opposed to *impelled redistribution through taxation*). As you will read in the ensuing chapters, large amounts of the consumer's budget will be diverted away from the establishment, and redistributed back to the consumer, creating an eventual win/win for all. With the successful implementation of these concepts and formulations, this *natural redistribution* model would occur through the mortgage and debt finance industry, through a new healthcare approach, and more critically, within the new *tax-free, no-market-loss* retirement structure.

Disclaimer

Unfortunately, I was first exposed to finance in the realm of *get-rich-quick* products and formulations of real estate with many of the big names in the intermountain region (Utah/Idaho/Nevada), during the 1980's. Signing on as an assistant to one of these "gurus". I quickly saw the fallacy in their concepts, yet simultaneously saw the masses fork over vast amounts of money for these *get-rich-quick* concepts.

Fortunately, those two short years of hobnobbing with the who's who in this *get-rich-quick* realm pushed me to the conservative side of the financial spectrum. Twenty-five years later, many of these "gurus" can still be seen pushing their wares on infomercials from three to five o'clock in the morning. Many have left the real estate realm and are now offering online investing (or similar packages) comprised of the same basic formulation: *get rich quick* at a *high risk* and a *high cost.* From firsthand experience (and in listening in on their call-center conversations), I can confidently state that most of these tactics are nothing short of extreme exploitation of the financially under-educated.

> [Side Bar: My swing to conservative finance did not mean settling for slow growth or low yields, but quite the contrary. As you will see, this innovative yet conservative approach to finance enables the average American to pay-off 5 to 10 homes in the same time it takes to pay off just one in our current archaic system.]

In the ensuing thirteen years I was employed at a printing firm, which provided me the opportunity to read a lot of material we printed on the latest and greatest financial concepts of that time. A big personal payoff was the experience of playing a role in growing that small print operation into a Fortune 500 firm. The experience of planning, projecting for growth, production flow, etc. (via ISO 9002) was irreplaceable. I would not have gotten this far in my current endeavors without that experience.

In the late 90's I was fortunate enough to form a partnership with an individual who was dabbling in the multimedia industry. In this venture we configured an innovative multimedia format and began offering a new approach to computer-based education and marketing.

Getting My Feet Wet in Finance

Being in Utah, it is probably no surprise that one of my first multimedia clients was a multi-level marketing firm (MLM). It was an innovative health supplement firm that was looking for a new, fresh style of marketing. After a few short months one of my multimedia productions landed on the desk of one of the nation's leading CEOs who had teamed up with two other well-known CEOs to form a financial education company.

> [Side Bar: These CEOs were Bill Fields (Wal-Mart Stores); Steve Smith (Excel Communications—noted for being one of the fastest growing companies in U.S. history, without pooling funds/assets from acquisitions); and, Steve Gurasich (GSD&M Advertising Agency—one of the noted top five in the nation).]

The purpose of this educational firm was to *solve America's debt crisis*. It was said in the 1990's that Wal-Mart was averaging a 12% share of the discretionary income of American households. In the years following the 9/11 attacks, however, this average dropped substantially when Americans began using their discretionary income to pay down debt, rather than spending it at Wal-Mart. Therefore, if they could educate Americans on how to get out of debt more quickly and efficiently, Wal-Mart could once again realize the share of discretionary income it had previously enjoyed.

Though the ideas of this financial education company were innovative and somewhat progressive, they did not vary too much from the basic financial concepts taught for decades. Hence, it was still an *old school* approach that neither showed large yields, nor addressed the basic structural flaws of the financial culture of the U.S. banking/financial system.

These individuals (Fields, Smith, and Gurasich) have my full regard and applause for literally *putting the consumer first* in their business model. It was a pleasure to work with these men of great integrity, and quite reassuring and refreshing in the aftermath of the Enron, WorldCom, Arthur Anderson, and other corporate scandals.

After my experience with this Texas-based company, I was the recipient of a little piece of paper that was about to have a notable impact on my future.

This particular piece of paper was comprised of no more than four square-inches, crookedly printed with black faded ink in the most ugly font in the digital age (Courier); and, the tape used to adhere the little square flier to my door had a dirty fingerprint in the adhesive, which was very apparent when taped on my white door. The message, however, came across loud and clear:

> Pay your home off in 1/3rd the time or less without increasing your income. Save 10's of 1000's of dollars in mortgage interest.

Though it sounded too good to be true, as things of this nature usually do, I wanted to hear what this salesman had to say. I have always maintained an open mind for new ideas, as you never know which one will pay off. This one did.

I asked an employee to step into the meeting with me so that I could have two minds assessing the presentation, just in case something got past one of us. I recall, to this day, the overwhelming response we had to this salesman's presentation, despite the fact that he struggled with its newness as it had only hit the mainland less than a year before.

> [Side Bar: I use the word *mainland* because the actual concept came from New Zealand by those familiar with the Australian banking system. They initially took the concept to Hawaii. I wasn't aware of the *origin of the concept* at first. It was under a much different circumstance that "the history of its origin" was later divulged, which I will explain momentarily.]

Throughout the meeting with this salesman, my employee and I were continually aghast with this thought, "How could this concept have gone so long without discovery?" Dazed and in complete awe, I decided to use my educational media to educate others on the concept. It was my intention to join the firm, but as it turned out, we were too incompatible.

Still, I felt that the concept was still worth pursuing. Within a week I received a phone call from either Mike or Norm at the *Norm & Mike Radio Program* out of Los Angeles. (I believe they had received one of my educational CD-ROMs.) We had extensive talks over a seven-day period therein discovering that they too were disappointed with the originating company. (I am still impressed with Norm & Mike. I always appreciate straight shooters.)

> [Side Bar: It is crucial that the public knows how this concept is being marketed, the specific methods that are now being employed, but most importantly, *how* you (the consumer) can decipher the signs of either a good provider or a scam provider. Where there were only four players in the industry in 2003-2004, today there are numerous companies offering these services, some of which are scams, which is evidenced by their approach, their structure, and their Standard Operating Procedures.]

Shortly after signing on with the originating company, I came across insider information that it was releasing a *do-it-yourself* software program at approximately one sixth of the cost, undercutting its own franchisees.

If I am not mistaken Norm & Mike were negatively impacted by this maneuver, and they came up with their own math engine to undercut the original do-it-yourself under-cutters. When this happened, the original salesman divulged more history of the company and sent me to the sister company located in Hawaii.

As presented to me, the two founders of the company were in-laws who did the majority of their configuring in New Zealand and Hawaii. There was reportedly a falling out, after which one of them relocated to Las Vegas, while the other stayed in Hawaii under a different company name and marketing concept.

After reformatting my multi-media production to reflect the new company and its varying nuances, I began attracting clients to this Hawaii-based firm, which was structured in a loose commission-based sales model. Very quickly, however, I came to appreciate the value of a <u>*precise math engine*</u>.

During these early years, the Option-ARM mortgage (or Negative Amortization Mortgage) was the *mortgage flavor of the week*, which actually grew out of the popularized yet flawed financial concepts of those years: *Never Pay Your Home Off,* but instead *Invest the Difference from an Interest Only Loan.*

Unfortunately, the math engines employed by these first two mortgage acceleration companies were only geared to *fixed mortgages* and not the *interest-only mortgages,* a big difference if one is trying to both accelerate the mortgage pay down <u>and</u> project *when* the home would be paid off and *how much* mortgage interest the homeowner would save on the program in order to feasibly justify "paying for the product" (*i.e.* calculating the *Return on Investment*).

As a result of their math engine inaccuracies, the sales approach quickly became the typical *bait and switch*. When discovering the inaccuracies of these engines, the company's response was,

"It really doesn't matter how much the client saves because we are saving them so much money anyway." Having created two very expensive multimedia productions for these two originating firms at my expense, I realized what I needed was an *accurate* math engine as I was personally endorsing this product.

I gave this second firm the option of correcting its math engine within six months, or else I would have to set off on my own to create those engines. The principals (who I maintain to this day are upstanding individuals) informed me that they were not going to retool the math engine. With my lost investments in the marketing productions for these two originating companies, I set off in a new direction, creating a company and a new math engine. What transpired over the ensuing ten years, as you will see, has become a phenomenal journey of discovery.

Perfecting the Concepts

Over the next 18 months, I submersed myself in calculators and mortgage tables. It was a crash course in finance. Never had I focused so intently on one subject or one project. For months on end (often 20 hours per day) I did nothing but eat, sleep, and breathe numbers, integrating them in and out of spreadsheets and databases, without leaving my home office for weeks at a time.

During this period I was also working closely with various mortgage loan officers, bankers, financial planners, and CPAs, having them challenge both my work and the premises of the formulations.

Simultaneously, I approached an old acquaintance from a separate, earlier, venture in the insurance industry. Having heard of the mortgage acceleration concept, he was interested in configuring a way to employ the tax-free benefit of insurance as an investment or retirement vehicle, using the mortgage accelerator as the springboard for aggressively funding a safe, tax-free retirement once the consumer debt was paid off and the mortgage was either paid off or close to being paid off, depending on the age and the status of each individual.

For months, we dovetailed a variety of insurance products into the mortgage accelerator math concept, configuring the schedule of transfers with a conservative rate of growth, which provided a much more productive, much less government-regulated tax-free retirement, or as we have come to call it, a tax-free, *deferred income* retirement. The mechanics of *deferred income* are completely juxtaposed to the mechanics of the failed *deferred tax* vehicles. Within months, we found and focused in on what has become the most effective and secure *tax-free, deferred income* vehicle currently on the market. (Details of this are found in chapter 7.)

Within the first year, we identified two flagship products that (when coupled together) created not only a whole new mindset in the financial realm, but also a whole new behavioral set—a whole new way of living and banking.

Unfortunately, these two products brought us head to head not only with our mortgage acceleration competition, but also with CPAs, accountants, securities-based financial planners, and bankers.

Within weeks our concepts were challenged by The Senior Annuity Center, a firm in Layton, Utah, headed by an inquisitive CPA. He and two of his associates came to my home office to discuss these new-fangled financial formulations.

After a two-hour discussion in my home office, I was invited to their offices to present these concepts in what became an extended-staff meeting of security brokers, attorneys, CPAs, accountants, bankers, and a mortgage broker. The scheduled 90-minute meeting evolved into a 6-hour, in-depth discussion of these new financial formulations.

It was at this point that I realized the magnitude of what I had to offer the general public. The following soon became my trademark *personal invitation* to all prospective clients:

> *If I am able to save you $164,000* (the average mortgage-interest savings of my clients), *why not pay your CPA or a trusted accountant $100 to come in and do the due diligence for you?*

Immediately, the prospective clients began bringing their CPAs, accountants, and financial advisors to my office. At first, they attempt to reduce the concepts and formulations to *smoke and mirrors,* holding on to the belief that the results can simply be accomplished by putting your extra money against the mortgage.

Once I present the math, they would state, "It's too complex. It is going to take a lot of handholding, and much discipline." After an hour or so of discussion, they typically come to see the simplicity, commonsense, and quantifiable logic of these concepts, and usually align their mindset and their practices with ours.

I can state factually that our greatest growth, even during our *Research & Development* phase, has come through these very CPAs who have sent (and continue to send) their clientele base to us for processing them into the new financial system, which system thrives within the current American financial structure.

Scams in Every Industry

In the seemingly countless and never-ending discussions I have had with just about every player in both the mortgage accelerator and related financial industries, I have come across countless scams regardless of the presence of government regulators.

This isn't so much a *complaint*, as much as it is a *call to opportunity.* I once had a business mentor state, "*Ron, in America, if you can change the direction of a large industry just one small degree, that small change will create a vacuum of opportunity."*

One way to change the direction of an industry requires the identifying and exposing scam-type elements within that industry, and then providing solutions to those. Depending on the number and depth of the scams, an industry can be completely reversed in its direction. If this happens, the opportunities are almost endless.

From what I have both seen and experienced in the mortgage, banking, mortgage financing, retirement, and insurance industries, there are some rather large changes in order, indicating much opportunity for many.

Within the mortgage acceleration industry itself, many of the providers present the façade that you *must* refinance your home in order for the mortgage acceleration concept to work properly or more efficiently. With very few exceptions, you seldom, if ever, have to refinance your home for these concepts to work.

Moreover, a few of the mortgage acceleration providers claim that you should be on the true Australian *Variable Interest-Only* mortgage, wherein your paycheck can literally sit against your mortgage. But, don't fall for that line, and don't let anyone convince you otherwise.

By employing the use of everyday banking products, and using the Home Equity Line of Credit (HELOC) as the *buffer account* (which will be explained in detail), it is much more efficient using smaller increments of a HELOC to transfer against the mortgage, rather than to have your entire first mortgage riding on a variable interest-only mortgage, as the "Australian Mortgage" providers are claiming. It is not only more expensive in the short term (*even if interest rates stay reasonably low*), but it's also more risky in the long run. In just a few cycles of a down-turned economy, you could lose big. (This will make much more sense after reading the ensuing chapters.)

There is a Better Way

I dare to say that not only has this information been made difficult for the masses to obtain, but the masses have been conditioned to stay in debt. For the most part, Americans have gained their entire financial education from mom and dad, based on *their* lack of financial understanding or prowess, which *lack was* inherited for generations before. The financially under-educated masses of America have been a prime target of usury on a macro-economic scale throughout history. Again, the institutions of higher education have done little (if anything) to improve our general lack of financial education.

The last eight years of research, market development, and market penetration have enabled me to assert with confidence: There *is* a better way.

When you make the physical and mental transition from the financial vehicles that were created back when we were on the gold standard (*i.e.* savings accounts and checking accounts) into the newer, more efficient financial vehicles of the current electronically-based fiat economy, you will have a clearer understanding of the terms *becoming your own bank, living in the buffer account, having instant access to all of your equity, no fear of foreclosure, lawsuit protection,* and *having the ultimate financial safety net…*to name a few.

When you have successfully made the transformation, a whole new world of finance will emerge before you—far from the old ways of *defensive* finance where you are continually climbing out of the pit of debt. These new concepts enable you to operate from a position of *offensive* finance.

Chapter 2: The Mortgage Acceleration Industry

Chapter 3: The Mortgage Acceleration Industry

In the Australian banking system, mortgages are structured in such a manner that no matter how much "extra" money a person pays against his mortgage, he can always pull it back out at any time. Better stated, he always has access to the equity in his home without having to qualify for it, let alone pay to get it out (via refinancing fees).

Obviously, this creates a double-edged sword: On the positive side, you could pay extra money against the mortgage without having to worry about getting laid off or injured, thereby avoiding the risks of foreclosure; on the negative side, consumers who are prone to over-spending money when they have a readily available line of credit might use it unwisely.

Also, because these mortgages are open-ended (meaning, the balance fluctuates like a credit card), they more often than not carry a variable interest rate. In my opinion, for the most part, a variable interest rate on a large-ticket item (such as a mortgage) is too risky, and even dangerous, for the majority of the population.

In my nine years of educating on these principles, I have found that having access to one's equity creates no temptation when the client sees that the total pay-off period of the mortgage is less than ten years. As a matter of fact, it is the unparalleled enthusiasm toward actually reaching that goal, which overrides the temptation to spend this readily accessible money.

Some feel that staying on these types of *programs requires a considerable amount of discipline.* For the vast majority of my clients, this is simply not true. Both *temptation to spend* and the *self discipline to stay on the program* are replaced by *enthusiasm for the goal.* When clients see how fast the pay-off is for consumer debt, student loans, and for their mortgage, the positive forces of *enthusiasm* kick in, and the *self discipline* is bolstered. The lifestyle is *positive*.

With a new financial foundation and a vastly different financial outlook, behavioral modification occurs naturally. In meeting with people, I have witnessed husbands turn to wives and state, "I am going to start taking a sack lunch to work", out of enthusiasm, rather than out of *need* or *dread.* It happens instantaneously because these people realize they can cut the pay-off time of the mortgage from 7 years and 6 months down to 6 years and 11 months with simple modifications in their financial paradigms and behaviors.

That said, we now have the task of manipulating some of the over-the-counter banking products in the U.S. banking system, to mimic the Australian mortgage structure.

The U.S. banking system is comprised of checking accounts, savings accounts, certificates of deposits (savings accounts with hand-cuffs), personal loans, home loans (mortgages), home equity lines of credit (HELOCs), credit cards, debit cards (an easier way to obtain money from your checking account), and a plethora of services (and non-services) for which banks can charge you fees.

Interestingly, one of the first competing providers of mortgage acceleration in the U.S. market configured an interest-only mortgage with an auto-sweep function to better mimic the Australian system. This function enabled the cash of the checking account to automatically sweep into the mortgage where it stayed until the homeowner needed that cash to pay for living expenses. To access those funds, he simply wrote a check wherein the funds were pulled from the mortgage, increasing the balance of the mortgage.

However, the Australian system is not as efficient as employing the use of everyday U.S. banking products in the correctly configured manner. When structured properly, these new configurations can be used with *any* mortgage product. So, again, if a mortgage-acceleration provider is pitching the concept that *you must refinance with them using their special mortgage*, consider it a red flag.

In the true Australian mortgage system, your entire 1st mortgage becomes, in essence, a HELOC. You do not want \$100,000 to \$1,000,000 sitting in a variable interest-only mortgage for very long, subject to the interest-rate swings, depending on the economy and depending on your ability to move it into a lower-interest vehicle should the rate rise.

Bottom Line: I have run many client profiles through both methods, side-by-side. In all real-life models, the Australian-based, interest-only mortgages cannot compete with the buffer account/HELOC method, either in pay-off time or interest savings. For those who don't know exactly what I'm talking about, allow me to qualify the term *real-life model*.

Real-Life Model: There are cases where the variable interest-only mortgage may compete with the buffer account approach of the HELOC, such as when the mortgage balance is low, say, \$50,000 or lower. But in real life, those mortgages are few and far between. Additionally, if someone's mortgage has been paid down to the \$50,000 level, they are most likely on the tail end of a 30- or 15-year fixed mortgage wherein the interest portion of the monthly payment is relatively low, and where the overall savings by accelerating the mortgage becomes somewhat negligible.

> [Side Bar: Most homeowners with an interest-only mortgage are in this type of mortgage simply to reduce payments so they have extra money to go

invest, or play, or save. Or, they are only going to be in the home for a short period of time. They generally are not interested in paying down the mortgage quickly.]

So, for those who have paid their mortgage down to the $50,000 level, regardless of mortgage type, why would a company (or financial planner) have them pay $5,000 to refinance into the Australian mortgage, when they could simply obtain the HELOC at no cost, and then pay down the $50,000 as quickly (or more quickly) than on the Australian-type mortgage?

In reality, only 5% of my clients ever need to refinance to make the system work for them, which is a great segue into the next section—The refinance scam (as marketed by the newcomers in the industry). Many providers are mimicking the Australian system in an attempt to create mystique, uniqueness, or novelty as a marketing strategy, needlessly gouging the consumer with refinancing costs.

Mortgage Acceleration Providers: Mortgage Brokers

Let me reiterate: If you are required to refinance your mortgage in order to participate in an acceleration program, you have the wrong provider.

There have been a number of mortgage brokers who have either obtained a simple mortgage accelerator calculator (or teamed up with someone who has a math engine) started a company, and in their marketing approach require, or strongly suggest that you refinance with them *to make the system work better for you*.

In this manner they collect their fee for the mortgage acceleration while supplementing their mortgage business through the mortgage fees. Just know that whenever refinancing is being presented as a requisite for making the mortgage acceleration "work properly", with very few exceptions, this is false.

[Side Bar: I also have a problem with mortgage brokers, the vast majority of loan officers, and pretty much the entire mortgage industry as a whole based on what I call my personal 3-strikes-out-of-3 experience in this industry. In 3 closings on 3 mortgages, I was "rated up" at the closing table. On the third incident, I objected and walked from the table. The mortgage broker recanted and rewrote the loan as originally configured.

Because of this 3-strikes-out-of-3 experience, I produced a multi-media presentation exposing the lender's *yield spread premium* (YSP) game.

With the large gains that come from the Yield Spread Premium structure, it is no surprise that we had the 2008 mortgage meltdown. Mortgage brokers (and loan officers) have big cash incentives from mortgage financiers to increase the *points* via the YSP. This YSP incentive, coupled with the attractively low *introductory rates* of 1% to 3% mortgages of the popular Option ARM mortgages (Adjustable Rate Mortgages) created *the perfect mortgage storm.* History will prove that this mortgage configuration will rate right up there with the S & L scam of the 1980's, all under the watchful eye of federal regulatory agencies.]

Providers with Inaccurate Math Engines

The math engine is probably the most critical element that a mortgage acceleration provider brings to the table. After all the algorithms have run their course, the actual output consists of simple, table-based schedules that can easily be verified with rudimentary eighth-grade math skills.

Any provider's math engine should also be able to account for *temporary* as well as *futuristic* income and expenses while providing a quick traceable history of the account activities. For example, let's say you are a single mother with three children for whom you are receiving child support. In three years, your oldest child turns 18, and the child support for that child ends. In

5 years as the second child turns 18, your income will drop again. And then, when the third child turns 18, you will lose all child support.

Conversely, as these children turn 18, the parent who is paying the child support no longer has the child-support expenses, and as the expense decreases, the discretionary income increases. These factors have an incredible impact on the pay-off scheduling, as well as on the overall savings. If your provider's math engine(s) will not account for these crucially dynamic factors, you have the wrong provider.

Also, as I mentioned, the ability to track the history of the account is crucial for the overall strategy. Most *do-it-yourself* mortgage acceleration calculators only provide a "snapshot" in time: A *snapshot* does not provide you the financial history of *where you have been*, and therefore, the providers of these types of calculators have no choice but to sell their service with *bait n' switch* tactics. If you can't track what has happened, there is no proving what the pay-off time or the interest savings will be; nor is it possible to hold the provider's feet to the fire for errant projections (ergo, bait n' switch).

It is for this reason that my firm (and those firms who contract with me to provide these services structured to my specifications) can offer a money back guarantee if we cannot achieve the projections we provide you at the onset of the program. The money back guarantee takes into account changes in the client's financial profile. At every change in the client's finances, we recast the projections and the guarantee is based on the recast projections.

Providers with Do-It-Yourself Calculators

There are many providers offering a *Do-It-Yourself* calculator for $200 to $500. I have many prospective clients who went that route, then later approached me to help them with the restructuring of their accounts and banking practices. If you are financially or mathematically inclined, you can most likely figure out the transition. But chances are you are not going to sit down, calculate and reconfigure your finances each time they change.

Therefore, an efficient math engine must be fluid enough to change, or be updated often; such as when Johnny and Suzie start or stop soccer, piano lessons, and day care creating an extra $50/month in outflow; or, when you get a tax return, or have to pay taxes; when you get a raise or demotion. In essence, whenever your finances change in the least degree, the math engine must have the capacity to maintain the history, and accurately re-project the future schedules, savings, and pay-off period(s). Changes to your finances will affect your rate of transfers between the accounts and, therefore, will change your payoff date and overall savings on the program.

As I have often stated to my clients, you can learn how to do taxes, but it is generally more cost effective to have an accountant do them for you. In this case, if you are anything like my average client, your mortgage interest savings will be $164,000 over a 9-year period, or about $18,000 per year. Hint: Hire the professional at roughly the cost of 1/6th the savings of just one of those 9 years (as most of these packages run from $3,000 to $4,000).

> [Side Bar: Price may be a key factor in the decision-making process for selecting a provider. However, in reality, a $3,000 to $4,000 price tag for a $164,000 savings over a 9 year period (again, based on my clients' average) creates approximately 4100% return on investment (ROI), or a 450% ROI for the first year.]

The price of the mortgage acceleration products/services has decreased in recent years. Currently, our firm is at the point of offering mortgage acceleration at no charge as a value-added service within an employee benefits package.

In my nearly 9-year history in the mortgage acceleration trenches, I have found that the savings do not stop with mortgage acceleration. When you have acquired the full picture of what is now available, you will be paying much less for other big ticket items such as cars, student loans, and other items you normally finance. (I discuss this in the section entitled *Becoming Your Own Bank* at the end of Chapter 4.)

Invest-the-Difference Providers

In the 1980s, there was a tremendous push by A.L. Williams that changed the insurance/investment industries drastically (and not all for the good). The concept was, *buy term* (life insurance) *and invest the difference*.

With this configuration, consumers would unload their whole life or cash-value policies that carried substantially higher monthly premiums (as these policies contained an investment aspect). They would then replace these cash value policies with the cheaper term insurance policies, thereafter investing the difference in the stock market—a much more volatile investment.

> [Side Bar: You will see in Chapter 7 *Tax-Free Deferred Income*, that because of the dramatic effect of terrorism on the stock market, AND because of mega-scandals (such as the WorldCom, Enron, and Madoff) involving corrupt and inept government and Wall Street entities, we have come full circle; namely, returning to insurance vehicles for retirement supplementation and for tax-free deferred income. With the new insurance vehicles on the insurance smorgasbord, this is quickly becoming the wave of the future for safe, sound, tax-free retirement strategies, but ONLY if the insurance is configured to the benefit of the consumer.]

The point of this section is to expose how this *buy-term-and-invest-the-difference* approach to insurance has been imported into the accelerated mortgage arena, adding to the devastating mortgage crisis in which we now find ourselves.

There are two large companies in the market pushing the concept of obtaining a minimum monthly payment or negative amortization (neg-am) mortgage (often called the Option ARM mortgage). These mortgages are structured in such a manner that you pay "the minimum required payment" and take the difference and put it into the stock market or even into insurance.

The detrimental aspect of this approach is that the *minimum required mortgage payment* is far less than what the actual interest is. Hence, if the interest portion of your payment is $1,000, but the minimum required payment for the Option ARM (mortgage) is only $250, this means the bank would be losing $750 per month. Is the bank going to lose $750 per month? No. The bank is not going to lose $750 per month: *You* will. When you pay your $250 payment, the shortage of $750 is actually added back on to your mortgage, ergo, the aptly named *negative amortization mortgage*. In this case, after paying your $250 payment on your $150,000 mortgage, the next month your mortgage balance is $150,750.00, because it is increased by $750 each month. Can you begin to see why we are having a mortgage meltdown? Whereas homeowners started with a $150,000 mortgage, 5 years down the road, they now have a $210,000 mortgage. Moreover, the $750/month that was invested in the stock market was also lost. Is it any wonder so many people are calling for redistribution of wealth through legislation and taxation?

Let me simplify this: Take the equity of your home and put it in the stock market. For those of you who are not dumbstruck with the gravity of this concept, I will restate it. Two major U.S. companies are pushing the concept of *taking the equity out of your home and going and gambling it on the stock market.* This is certainly no different from the government allowing employers to take money from your paycheck (via the 401k), wherein it, too, is gambled on the stock market. From my point of view, I see no difference in the gambling of home equity and the gambling of retirement funds. The stock market is no place for either your home equity or your retirement funds. After all, the first caveat that a stock broker offers an investor is, *Don't invest on the stock market unless you can stand to lose it.* (This concept is discussed in more detail in Chapter 7.)

The Option ARM mortgage is normally structured with an attractively low introductory interest rate of 1% for the first 12 to 18 months. Again, just because a loan has an *introductory rate* of 1% does not mean that you are meeting the minimum interest payment, but instead you are negatively amortizing (having debt added on to your mortgage each month). After 12 to 18 months, the mortgage then adjusts to a low rate of say, 4.5% until year 5 of the loan. After that, it adjusts to prime plus a certain margin above that (usually 1 to 3 percentage points), and increases in interest each year there.

> [Side Bar: These Option ARM mortgages are also characterized by containing "options" where the borrower has four different options of payment: 1) payment of the minimum introductory rate of 1%, 2) payment of the interest-only rate or all of the interest, 3) payment of the interest plus the principal of a 30-year amortization table, or 4) payment of the interest plus the principal of a 15-year amortization table.]

There are two cases or circumstances where I would recommend this, or similar interest-only type, mortgage: 1) If my client were in dire straits financially, heading for lay-off or other difficulty AND we knew he had job opportunities on the horizon; or 2) If the mortgage created substantially more discretionary income that would/could increase the mortgage acceleration cycles under the mortgage acceleration program where we could have the mortgage paid off or close to being paid off within the adjustment period.

For the vast majority of my clients, however, *if* they need to refinance, I will (more often than not) recommend the 10/30 or 15/30 Hybrid if you can obtain one. With the post-2008 meltdown and the ensuing Frank/Dodd legislation, these hybrid loans are more difficult to obtain.

Refinancing your home for a higher payment and a higher interest rate in order to take out cash to put into an investment device is still too radical for my taste, unless the amounts you are pulling out are very small, and are paid back quickly.

Marketing Structures of Various Providers

The marketing structure most likely will determine your experience in this new system. For example, the most notable firm that has established early market presence in the mortgage acceleration industry is a multi-level or network marketing firm, located in the state of Utah.

The multi-level marketing approach in this industry is counter to financial prudence. People cannot (and should not) trust Ma n' Pa up-line or down-line networkers for financial expertise or advice. It is the lack of Ma n' Pa's financial acumen that is responsible for our age-old misconceptions and errant financial practices. A key component for taking the mortgage acceleration concept forward is the inclusion of licensed financial professionals who are willing to put their license on the line or, at minimum, are bonded or insured against errors and/or omissions.

Including the Professionals

My current educational approach (which calls for the inclusion of financial professionals such as CPAs) has produced four overwhelming results:

1. The prospective clients came into the office, into the process, and into the discussion much more open minded and ready to learn;
2. These prospective clients immediately become clients, without hindering or altering their relationship with their CPA or financial planner;
3. The CPAs began sending in their other clients; and,
4. I began establishing a network of CPAs who have become familiar with the system, yet have relied on me (and my staff) to transition their clients into the new system.

This approach has benefitted all involved, which is why I continue to commence my seminars or educational series with the same invitation: *Please feel free to bring your CPA or trusted financial advisor with you to any and all meetings.*

Chapter 4: The Mortgage Acceleration Program

Through the years of merging the Australian concept with American banking, I have discovered that it is just as applicable to the lower and middle classes as it to the wealthy.

As I have quantified over the years, it is now possible to pay for five to ten properties in 30 years with this system, whereas we have been conditioned to pay off only one property in that same amount of time. This, in and of itself, creates much more wealth, or better yet, a substantial, robust estate for all financial classes much more quickly.

In the final section of this chapter entitled Multi-Property Acquisitions, I will provide an actual client case where the client was struggling to even pay the mortgages on his rental properties, let alone pay those mortgages off *early*. On the program, however, he is able to pay them all off in just over 23 years saving over $1.4M in mortgage interest.

The path I take in getting my clients started in this new financial direction closely reflects the typical financial life stages of an average American citizen, namely:

1. Finance/Mortgage Education
2. Consumer Debt Elimination
3. Mortgage Acceleration
4. Asset Protection
5. Estate/Investment/Retirement Planning (with tax-free distributions as our main objective)

This chapter will focus on mortgage acceleration, how and why this product works better in the U.S. than it does in Australia (its place of origin), and what is now possible through mortgage acceleration for all economic classes.

From Point A to Point B

The shortest distance between two points is a straight line.

I have found both peace of mind, logic, and even safety in the exercise of adding the conditional *unless* to stated or generally accepted *absolutes*. For example, let's use *quantum* physics:

The shortest distance between two points is a straight line, unless we take into account quantum physics, wherein point A and point B are connected by a worm hole, wherein the actual distance cannot be measured; only the time one enters point A and exits point B is measurable.

Even then, the factor of *time* can be warped or altered in the context of quantum physics. Actual travel *time* between point A and Point B is now faster, but the *distance* may be longer. Now the terms *easiest* or *most efficient* route, and even the term *shortest distance* all become subjective to the aims, goals and desires of the traveler.

The *shortest distance* and *easiest way* are worlds apart when considering all possible factors.

In my opinion, it is this type of *unconditional* or *absolute* manner of thinking that is responsible for creating a century of errant conditioning in the financial realm. For example, we have been conditioned to think that if we want to pay our mortgage down more quickly, or go from a *large mortgage balance* (Point A) to *no mortgage balance* (Point B), we must unconditionally do one or more of the following:

1. Make more money and apply it to the mortgage.
2. Reduce our expenses and apply that extra money to the mortgage.
3. Refinance in order to reduce our interest rate.
4. Reduce our mortgage structure from a 30-year mortgage to a 15-year mortgage.
5. Enroll in a biweekly mortgage payment plan.

To all of this, I vehemently and profoundly state, “wrong!” There are *other* factors in play here. There is another way: a much better way.

Getting you from Point A to Point B of this mortgage acceleration puzzle is a cakewalk, not quantum physics or even wormhole travel. However, the mortgage acceleration question is just the first piece of the larger financial quandry.

Before laying out an individual financial plan, you must first consider your overall financial objectives, including your current status (and future projections) for retirement as discussed in detail in the section entitled *Tax-Free Deferred Income* in Chapter 7.

Do you want to get rid of the mortgage? Are you working on retirement? Are you getting massive taxes back each year, or are you paying taxes each year? And most importantly, how will accelerating your mortgage pay-down affect your retirement plan?

Instead of delving into the details of these questions at this point, I will explain them in their respective chapters.

Should I Pay Off My Home?

There are two schools of thought that say it is good to keep your mortgage: 1) Those who claim that you need to take the equity out of your home to invest it for growth, and 2) Those who claim it is best to hold on to the mortgage for the mortgage-interest write off.

Let's spend a minute recapping the fallacy of keeping the mortgage for the sake of the mortgage-interest tax shelter: You do not want a tax write-off where you are paying $1,000 per month to the bank so that you can create a $300 savings (if you are in the 30% tax bracket; or, a $200 savings if you are in the 20% tax bracket). That is a $700 to $800 net loss.

However, *if* I were able to get a tax write-off for $1,300 from the IRS for the $1,000 house payment, *then* I might consider whether that type of write-off is worth staying in debt. Barring that, pay your home off, and then pay your taxes of $300 (or go find another tax shelter for that $300): Take the remaining $700 and go play, or invest it, or send it to the poor and get a tax write-off for it. Once again, not having to make the payment at all is much better than what the mortgage-interest write-off could ever create.

Now, to address *delaying the paying off of your mortgage for years, so that you can invest the money*: My first response to this concept is *it depends on what the investment is*. If it is basic stock market investments, I resoundingly state, "No."

If it is insurance, I again resoundingly state, "No", although, in my opinion, insurance (if configured correctly) can be one of the best investments—just not with the equity of your home. I would typically be in favor of investing in *yourself* to improve your situation (*i.e.* career, employment, productivity, etc.).

Wall Street Investment with Home Equity

The vast majority of North Americans want to pay their home off. No questions asked. I have often said, "The American Dream isn't having a *mortgage*: It is owning your *home* and/or *land*."

Having lived through two of the nation's worst recessions, back to back within a 6-year period, in an era of prevalent terrorism, and in an unprecedented onslaught of corporate, Wall Street, and government corruption, I am amazed that we (Americans) continue to take our retirement dollars, and even the equity of our homes, and gamble them on the stock market in the presence of such volatility (risk).

For example, **IF** three more planes hit three more buildings resulting in the shutdown of ALL air travel for three days resulting in another 50% loss of my retirement fund (because that fund was directly tied to the stock market); and whereas after more than a decade, I still haven't gained it all back, **THEN**, why oh why would I want to subject any more of my retirement dollars to this type of market loss?

In reality, we need not wait for the next terrorist attack because there are also other factors working against the stock market-based 401(k)s, IRAs, or SEPs; such factors as Enron, WorldCom, FNMA, Freddie Mac Mortgage, etc. In a way, I am more concerned about the factors of corruption and ineptness on the part of Wall Street and the U.S. government than I am about any other factors that create stock market volatility (like calamities, terrorism, or negative *consumer*, *unemployment*, or *housing-starts* quarterly reports).

The bigger question relative to this chapter, however, is this: If I am uncomfortable subjecting my retirement dollars to stock market loss, then why would I want to take the equity out of my home and subject it to the same volatility and risk factors? The qualifiers of whether or not you participate in these "retirement" vehicles can be summed up and easily analyzed with two simple questions: 1) Can I stand to lose my funded retirement? 2) Can I stand to lose my home equity?

If the answers to these questions are "yes", then this book is probably not for you. If your answers are "no", chances are you now have (or soon will have) many more questions; namely, what should I do? How and when should I do it? Where do I go from here?

Unless there are other factors in your finances (that I have not yet discussed) that would prevent you from accelerating your mortgage, I would recommend paying your mortgage off as quickly as possible. If you feel you have a unique scenario or condition that would keep you from paying off your mortgage (other than divorce strategies, legal limitations, or some outrageously long prepayment penalty clause), I would love to hear about it. I am looking to learn more, and both my door and mind are always open to discover new, unknown conditions and factors.

How It Works

The first step is to move from the cash-based account (your current checking account) into a debt-based account or *line of credit.* Though you can use any type of line of credit to make this work, I will use a HELOC (Home Equity Line of Credit) for illustration purposes only. To make this systemic jump, you will be doing a mental *one-eighty* in how you have been thinking and acting financially. Let me explain.

Picture a square with a human stick figure in it. This square represents a U.S. checking account. The stick figure is the typical American who lives (financially) in the checking account. Otherwise stated, the checking account has been the center of our stick figure's financial universe.

Upon receiving her paycheck, our stick figure goes up to her waist in "dollar bills." Upon paying her mortgage, the level of dollar bills drops to knee level. In the ensuing weeks as she pays her other living expenses, the level of those remaining dollar bills drops down to her ankles, or lower. She is constantly looking down to see how many more dollars she has left to spend; she is always looking for the next check so that she can replenish the level of dollar bills back up to her waist.

For the ultra-conservative: If there are any dollar bills left over at the end of the month, she would normally transfer those dollars into a savings account, making 1% or so.

Now, move the stick figure from the checking account to the HELOC. In the HELOC, instead of going up to her waist in dollar bills, she now goes up to her waist in good debt, while taking the money and applying it against bad debt (normally consumer debt) or against the mortgage.

As her paychecks come in, the entire paycheck is deposited into the HELOC, lowering the debt level down to her knees. And, with another paycheck the debt level is lowered to ankle level.

All expenses (where possible) are paid with a credit card (as on a credit card our expenses can remain for 25 to 55 days interest free, enabling the HELOC balance to remain low, keeping the daily calculated interest low). She then pays the entire balance of the credit card before any interest is charged.

Each time the debt level reaches her ankles, she takes out another chunk of money from the HELOC and applies it against the 1st mortgage, and then brings in her entire paycheck to pay down the HELOC for, say, 20 days of the month. This cyclical banking not only has a massive impact on daily calculated interest, but also can be healthy for your FICO scores.

> [Side Bar: I must state that these banking behaviors *may be* conducive for a healthy FICO score, because Fair Isaac (the firm behind the system) is comprised of individuals who determine the ever-evolving policies, actuarial factors, and financial formulations that determine your credit score; and, they alone can change the rules at any time. Currently, at the time of this publication, the practices we employ generally help to improve or enhance your score. However, what may be favorable today may be less favorable tomorrow.]

If you can picture this, the debt-based structure is the exact opposite cycling of the cash-based structure, where instead of going up to your waist in dollar bills, you go up to your waist in good, temporary debt. When you run out of debt (in the

HELOC), you simply go back up to your waist in good, temporary debt. How do you do this? You write a check from the HELOC to your first mortgage. In this manner, you are forcing yourself to aggressively move forward on paying down the 1st mortgage.

Getting Started

First, we work with any banking institution that has online banking capabilities, enabling us to easily transfer money back and forth between the checking account and the HELOC.

As I have said, we still have a checking account. It no longer maintains the central role in your finances, but instead will be used for two minor purposes.

The first purpose of the checking account is to enable us to continue receiving our paychecks via electronic deposit from our employers as there is really no need to disrupt the economic flow in order to make the transition.

The second purpose of the checking account is to give us the ability to pay a vendor who doesn't accept credit card payments, such as church donations, piano teachers, etc.

Why do we want to use a credit card? So we can delay paying for our living expenses until the last possible day. Why put $3,000 in living expenses on the HELOC and be charged the daily calculated interest on that $3,000 each day, when we can put that $3,000 on a credit card, interest free, for up to 55 days? Then, we simply pay off the balance of the credit card each month before we are charged interest, enabling us to leverage interest-free funds against debt.

Don't worry. This is certainly not the explanation of how the system works. This was just my method of introducing all the components of the system.

The Nuts and Bolts

The first *cardinal rule* of this system:
NO MONEY IN THE CHECKING ACCOUNT

Why don't we want money in the checking account? Because money in the checking account does nothing for us. Leaving money in the checking account only serves the bank. Banks, like insurance companies, know how to make money. When they have funds deposited in their bank, they know how to take that money and make 20% to 30%, while paying you 1% for your savings account balance, or 0% for your checking account balance.

If you have $5,000 of net income hitting your checking account the first of each month, and your mortgage and living expenses are not due until the fourth week of the month, then you would have 20 to 25 days wherein this money could sit against debt. Simplistically speaking: If that $5,000 could sit against your $200,000 mortgage for 20 days of the month, and this could be repeated month after month after month, the savings (in terms of reducing mortgage interest) is phenomenal. In effect, it creates *reverse compound interest* for the benefit of the consumer.

With this foundation in place, let's get into the details. In doing so, I am going to use smaller, simpler numbers to keep the math easy. I will also simplify the timing.

Let's begin with a $100,000 balance remaining on our 30-year fixed mortgage with a net income of $5,000 per month. The mortgage payment is $1,000 and we have $3,000 in expenses. This would leave us with $1,000/month in discretionary income (income that is not allocated to any payment or bill).

At the beginning of the month before the paycheck comes in, we move $7,000 out of the HELOC (via online banking) and move it into the checking account. We will then write a check from the checking account for the $7,000 payable to ABC Mortgage Company (our 1st mortgage holder).

With this transfer of $7,000, we reduce our 1st mortgage balance of $100,000 to $93,000.

[Side Bar: If this were an *interest-only* mortgage, the actual mortgage payment would be reduced from $527 down to $493, or $34 less per month, based on a 6.5% interest rate. On a *fixed* mortgage, the amount going toward the principal portion of the payment increases by that same $34, while the interest portion would be reduced by that amount.

Though this doesn't appear to be a big reduction right off the bat, after a few of these transfer cycles, it really starts to add up. Within a year, we expand this interest reduction to $100/month, and it just continues accelerating from that point. Generally speaking, if you are able to apply your entire paycheck to your mortgage for 20 days (or two-thirds) of the month, your overall mortgage payoff savings will somewhat reflect that ratio, reducing the life of our mortgage by about two-thirds.]

Getting back to our example: In creating a balance of $7,000 in our HELOC and moving it to the 1st mortgage, we create a $49 payment (at an 8.5% interest rate) in the HELOC. However, that is $49 if we have a $7,000 balance for the entire month. But guess what? We don't have a $7,000 balance for the entire month. Just after the check cleared our account from ABC mortgage for the $7,000, our paycheck of $5,000 came in, reducing our HELOC balance from $7,000 down to $2,000. This makes our HELOC payment $9.32 for the $2,000 for 20 days, and $13.97 for our balance of $6,000 for the last 10 days of the month. Keep in mind: We didn't have to return up to the $7,000 balance because we have $1,000 of discretionary income that can continue to sit against the HELOC.

In reality, we don't have to increase to the $6,000 balance on day twenty either, because the majority of the $3,000 living expenses can sit on the credit card for another 25 to 55 days without interest. That way we could keep the HELOC balance at roughly $3,000 for the entire month. At the beginning of the second month, another $5,000 paycheck comes in, and we are able to wipe out the $3,000 balance, thereby enabling us to start another cycle.

The second *cardinal rule* of this system is:

PUT ALL EXPENSES POSSIBLE ON THE CREDIT CARD AND LET THOSE EXPENSES STAY ON THE CREDIT CARD UNTIL THE DUE DATE; THEN PAY THE BALANCE OF THE CREDIT CARD FROM THE HELOC.

Whenever we come close to zeroing out the HELOC, we start another cycle by taking another chunk of money from the HELOC (increasing the HELOC balance) and applying that chunk to the 1st mortgage.

Cyclical Banking

Having a HELOC as your primary financial account opens up a whole new world of finance.

As explained in Chapter 2, the risk of foreclosure, for the most part, is removed. Your HELOC (with substantial equity) becomes your safety net. If you don't have substantial equity in the HELOC, the program will accelerate the process of creating equity, thereby rapidly establishing your safety net.

The safety net aspect of the program now overrides the purpose of the old savings account. Pulling from a previous example, if I have $40,000 in a savings account earning 1%, yet I pay 7% on my mortgage, I would realize an instant 6% on that $40,000 if I were to move that money over to the 1st mortgage.

If the purpose of the savings account is to serve as a rainy-day fund or a safety net, AND we have $100,000 available to us through the HELOC at the writing of a check, then the HELOC can serve as the safety net. And, as long as we never have a rainy-day need, we are earning 6% on that $40,000, which we moved from the 1% savings account against the 7% mortgage. If we do have to use that money for a rainy day, it will simply slow down the accelerated mortgage program.

Additionally, if we don't have a rainy-day need, and we are able to continue with the scheduled pay-down cycles, we will continually expand the HELOC as we buy down the first mortgage.

Two possible arguments against this approach might be 1) What if the market crashes and/or the bank changes its HELOC policies, thereby barring me from getting the money out of my home? 2) What if the economy crashes? I am at least covered for up to $100,000 in the savings account via FDIC.

Argument 1: True and Possible.
Argument 2: Not if more than 1.25% of the U.S. banks fail.

Yes, in a worst-case scenario, the bank could change its policy on HELOCs and could choose not to lend out funds through the HELOC—we have seen this in the wake of Black October 2008.

However, comparing apples to apples in the same worst-case scenario with an economic meltdown, your savings account is lost, as the FDIC (as you will see in chapter 7) does not, nor will it ever have the necessary funds to cover more than an approximated 1.25% of all bank accounts that are supposedly insured for up to $100,000 for individuals and $250,000 for couples. In a semi-worst-case scenario, the best you can hope for would be 10 cents on the dollar.

Therefore, given the worst-case scenario, would you rather lose your funds to the bank through FDIC failure (which is the current status of FDIC in a meltdown), or would you rather have that money in your home (against your mortgage)? Yes, there are many options out there to ready yourself for a "worst-case scenario", such as precious metals, cash in the mattress, etc., all of which carry their own risks.

As I have come to realize, however, you can't live your life (nor plan for the future effectively) based on worst-case scenarios, but you can strike the balance while hedging the odds against those worst-case scenarios. Owning your home outright hedges those odds in your favor tremendously. The clients who have established a robust equity footing in their homes have healthy HELOCs that reflect that equity. They have sailed through this recession unscathed, even where banks have rampantly frozen consumer HELOCs.

The greatest payoff of this new structure is achieved when you are to the point of what I call *becoming your own bank.*

Becoming Your Own Bank

As I have already presented, our lifestyle is usually determined by our discretionary income, which is *the money we have left over after our house payment and living expenses are paid*.

When we Americans realize that we have discretionary income, it is usually depleted by *financing* THINGS. Because we are financially and emotionally locked into a 30-year mortgage, we subsequently finance our way into a lifestyle (or lack thereof).

In the new system, we avoid financing consumer goods, but instead finance them through the HELOC, enabling your entire paycheck to sit against the item that you paid for with the HELOC. When you need a car, we simply postpone the transfer cycles (scheduled to be paid against the 1st mortgage), and instead apply those transfer cycles to the car.

You go to the car lot and negotiate a deal with the car dealer for a lower price, as you are paying for the car outright with cash. In the vast majority of my client cases, a $30,000 car is paid off (through the HELOC) somewhere between 18 and 24 months, rather than the typical 48 to 60 months.

It is also very important to note that postponing the cycled transfers against the home (in order to pay the car off) *does not equate* to extending the pay-off of your home the same 18 to 24 months; instead, the house pay-off is normally extended out only 9 to 14 months. It is not a one-to-one extension ratio. (This will make more sense when you participate in a live seminar or webinar where you can experience the math and mechanics behind the system.) This is just one of the reasons why an accurate and flexible math engine is requisite in selecting a mortgage acceleration provider.

Understanding the Banker's Opposition

As explained in the *Introduction*, the bankers with whom I have worked personally know that under this program they are gaining multiple mortgages, rather than losing interest to the consumer from just one mortgage.

Still, there are some bankers who, despite the fact that I send them clients for HELOC business (their bread and butter), they attempt to talk those clients out of mortgage acceleration. Out of ignorance to these principles, my clients are often the recipients of errant banker advice:

1) *You can do something like this on your own; you don't need to pay a company to do mortgage acceleration*; and,
2) *We can do the same thing through bi-weekly payments*

To these establishment bankers I posed the following questions and concerns:

A) Your bi-weekly payment will only reduce the client's mortgage from 30 years down to 22 because the bi-weekly program affects daily calculated interest very little compared to full-scale mortgage acceleration, which reduces the average mortgage from 30 years down to 9.

B) Can/Will you provide your clients with a schedule that will create an average of $164,000 in mortgage interest savings?
C) Will you guarantee your projections by contract?
D) If you can provide this level of savings, how come you are not advertising it?
E) Isn't it fiduciarily wrong to mislead consumers against viable services verified and backed by CPAs, yet not offer an alternative, or show the client how to do it?

Multi-Property Acquisitions

Before expounding on the multi-property concept, keep in mind that I am not pushing you into the real-estate realm as a retirement strategy. Such an approach would put you in the taxable environment. I would rather have you start building a non-taxable estate (Chapter 7) or, at minimum, combining the two strategies of the non-taxable environment with the taxable environment (stock market, real estate, etc.).

I came across a scenario in Washington state where the multi-property owner had a mortgage on his primary home of $520,000, and a second mortgage on his primary home of $227,000. As this primary mortgage is an interest-only loan, with a payment of $2,275 per month, he will never pay it off, unless he applies extra money to the principal. However, this client also has another five properties as listed below:

	Balance	Interest	Payment
Property 2	$240,000	6.75%	$1,350
Property 3	$208,191	6.75%	$1,171
Property 4	$155,206	6.75%	$ 873
Property 5	$158,455	6.75%	$ 891
Property 6	$177,450	6.75%	$ 998

I am sure many of you are thinking, "How could he get the same interest rate on so many different properties?" I thought the same thing. However, this individual has a loan officer that was able to secure all of these non-owner occupied mortgages at the same rate.

It must be noted that each of these properties are structured on interest-only mortgages, meaning they will never be paid off. This individual cannot even convert these mortgages to fixed mortgages wherein a small portion of the payments are applied to principal because the payments would be too high. He simply doesn't have the cash flow to make the payments.

The rental income is pretty much meeting the mortgage payments, so he is banking on the property values going up (appreciation) so that at some point he can sell them off, and thereby make a profit.

> [Side Bar: This particular individual has fared well with his renter occupancy rate (creating sufficient rental income) to continue treading water. However, I have many clients who have engaged in multi-property acquisition under a *leverage-based* strategy, rather than an *equity-based* strategy. Those clients, whose personal income is completely expended each month, solely relying on rental income to meet the mortgage payment of their rentals (with little-to-no room for vacancy or renter default) have been falling by the financial wayside since Fall of 2007. The accelerated mortgage approach creates a safer and more profitable way to enable multi-property acquisition through *equity plateaus* with each acquisition. For those of you already leveraged beyond your comfort level on your multiple properties (relative to the economy), there are a few *restructuring* tactics that can be implemented, which may enable you to feasibly transition into this more conservative structure.]

With these unique concepts of mortgage acceleration, this individual can leave the interest-only mortgages in place and still pay all six mortgages off in approximately 23 years and 8 months. Outside of this approach, this client is scheduled to pay $2,787,628 in mortgage interest. (That is IF these mortgages were paid off within 30 years.) Since they are interest-only mortgages, he may not stay on a 30-year schedule. On our program, he is now going to pay only $1,374,752 in mortgage interest, saving him $1,412,875 because the properties will be paid off in 23 years and 8 months.

The following is the Cliff Notes version of his pay-off strategy:

> For starters, this client has about $45,000 in consumer debt. We will be paying that off in 18 months, at which point his monthly discretionary income will increase significantly.
>
> Using the mortgage acceleration concepts, we will transition cyclical units of approximately $11,225 against property 4. This property 4 will be paid off in **month 74.**
>
> After month 74, we have freed up the $873 mortgage payment to be applied to the HELOC cycles, allowing us to now place cyclical units of approximately $15,155 against property 5, which is paid off in **month 114**—freeing up that mortgage payment and taking us to property 6.
>
> We then start applying cyclical units of $18,950 against property 6 until **month 152**, when it is paid off. In month 153, we then start on property 3 with cyclical units of about $23,750 through **month 187**.
>
> After month 187, we are able to start on property 2, allotting cyclical units of about $34,000 through **month 216**. And, in month 217, we will begin paying off the $227,000 interest-only second mortgage on the primary residence.
>
> And, finally, in **month 244**, we are ready to start on the primary residence, at which point we are able to put approximately $44,000 in cyclical units against that mortgage—**paying it off 40 months later**.

I am sure there are many of you inquiring, "Why didn't he pay off his primary residence first? Wouldn't that be the conservative thing to do?" As I have said time and time again, every client is as unique as a fingerprint: No two are alike. And, this particular client wanted the rental homes paid off first in order to create more discretionary income sooner, relative to each debt.

Often times, I have dentists or doctors who want me to schedule their student loans to be paid off first, although student loans are one of the best debt devices a consumer can have (vis-à-vis the low monthly payment). However, some debts have more psychological value (or create more psychological baggage) than others. Though I always prioritize the best debt payoff strategy, I will always defer to the client's wishes. Often, various debts will be treated and configured differently in cases of divorce, bankruptcy, or where other nuanced factors become part of the overall picture.

In reality, this client will probably not make it out to year 10 before acquiring another property. He may come to the following conclusion: I have 5 properties paid off. I can now take 25% of each of the five properties to pay for another property outright, creating a phenomenal ROI with rental inflow, removed from any mortgage outflow; and, the income from this new property can easily pay down the small lines of credit that were taken on the other five properties.

We can assist you to schedule as conservatively or aggressively as you desire. Though my standard recommendation is *balance*, with this equity-based approach you are able to finance properties (or the majority of properties) through your own equity lines, thus *becoming your own bank.*

Chapter 5: Interest Rates (For the Most Part) Do Not Matter

Payment Performance Ratio

It might come as a surprise that interest rates are the most effective tool used against the consumer to *head them off at the pass* so to speak, or keep them heading in the wrong direction, though we have been conditioned to think that interest rates are the most crucial aspect of finance.

If we, as consumers, are offered an interest rate above 15%, it's bad; below 6% and we're in good shape. If we can get 0% interest, we are the ultimate champions of finance. However, the interest rate is the least understood, and by far, the most overrated aspect of finance with the sole exception of large-ticket items such as mortgages.

When meeting with clients, I like to illustrate the following on the whiteboard:

I have a client who once had a *discretionary income* of $500/month (residual income after the house payment, living expenses, and all other bills are paid). This client also had two loans. Both loans had a balance of $4,500: Loan #1 had an interest rate of 19.99%, while Loan #2 carried an interest rate of 6%.

After drawing out these two loans on the board, I ask the client, "Removing the interest from both loans: If I were to apply the $500 of discretionary income to one of these debts, how long will it take to pay off the first $4,500 debt?" They will answer, "9 months". This is correct. 9 months multiplied by $500 = $4,500.

I then ask, "Now let's bring in the interest: If I apply the $500 each month to the loan with a 19.99% interest rate attached, how much longer (over the 9 months) will it take to pay off this loan?"

The answers are all over the board from 15 months to 2 years. I then ask, "If we pay off the 6% loan first, how much longer (than the 9 months) will 6% interest take to pay off, with the $500 applied against it each month?" The answer is anywhere from 1 year to 18 months.

In reality, by applying the $500 each month to the 19.99% loan, it would be paid off in 9 months and 6 days, while the 6% loan would be paid off in 9 months and 2 days.

I then ask, "Which bill do we want to pay off first: the 19.99% loan or the 6% loan?" Predictably the clients would reply adamantly with, "The 19.99% loan."

I then psychologically push the client further into the "interest rate trap" by divulging the payments of each loan. The 19.99% loan is a *credit card* that had a $25/month payment, while the 6% loan is for an automobile, which had a $250/month payment.

I would then ask, "Why does the credit card company only want a $25/month payment?" The response is a resounding, "Because they don't ever want you to pay off the loan, so that they can make more interest from you."

I continue psychologically pushing the client into the "interest-rate trap" with, "Even if you only pay $25 per month for the rest of your life, you will never pay off the loan, which interest could reach upwards of $25,000. It is at this point that the client returns with, "Then we need to get that loan paid off now."

I then shatter the interest-rate paradigm with the simple fact that, in this case, the 19.99% credit card loan is the better of the two loans, and that we want to pay off the 6% loan first. Here's the train of thought:

Scenario 1—Investor
If I were an investor with these two loans, I would want to retain the 19.99% credit card loan and pay off the 6% car loan as soon as I could. As an investor, I want as many dollars lent to me as possible for the least amount of payment.

In this scenario, the credit card company is lending $4,500 for only $25/month—meaning, as an investor I am only paying $1 for every $180 lent to me. This makes for a 180-to-1 ratio for the credit card loan. In contrast, the 6% car loan carrying the $250/month payment only makes for an 18-to-1 ratio (or, for every $1 of payment, the bank is only lending me $18).

> Car: $4,500 divided by $250 payment = $18 lent to me per each dollar of payment.
>
> Credit Card: $4,500 divided by $25 payment = $180 lent to me per each dollar of payment

Most investors would much rather have a ratio of $180-to-$1 than $18-to-$1.

Therefore, in finance, the **payment amount** is just as crucial (if not more) as the interest rate. I have come to term this ratio factor as the *Payment Performance Ratio* (PPR).

Let's look at this same formulation as a *consumer with the objective of getting out of debt*.

Scenario 2—Consumer Trying to Get Out of Debt
If we pay off the 19.99% loan in the first 9-month period, we will have only freed up the $25/month payment at the end of the first 9 months, creating a discretionary income of $525, to then go and pay off the car loan at 6%.

If we were to pay off the 6% loan first, we will have freed up the $250/month car payment at the end of the first 9 months—creating a $750 discretionary income with which to pay off the 19.99% loan.

[Side Bar: In all actuality, paying off the 19.99% loan rather than the 6% loan first (in this client's case) was slightly more cost effective for the simple fact that we did not put the car loan "on hold". It was also being paid down at the rate of $250/month while paying down the 6% loan, thus reducing the principal amount of the 6% loan.

However, I have been able to negotiate with lending institutions (on behalf of a few clients) the freezing of payments for six to nine months at a time. Though interest still accrues on this debt, we are able to shift our attention to apply more money against less effective debts. In this economy (of the past 12 years), lending institutions are very open-minded.

More relevant in this client's case is the fact that for the slight difference in cost effectiveness (less than $30 over the 9-month period), when given the choice at the 9-month mark of having $525/month in discretionary income or having $750/month in discretionary income, my clients overwhelmingly opt for *more discretionary income sooner* for the peace of mind and/or for the safety-net factor of having the larger monthly financial burden removed.]

Also, this scenario has a substantial interest rate spread between 19.99% and 6%. As this rate spread decreases, such as a 13% credit card loan and a 9% car loan, the interest rate becomes less and less important—and, for the most part, becomes a non-factor. *Freeing up more cash <u>sooner</u>* is paramount (in most cases).

The 0% Interest Temptation

The errant *interest-rate conditioning* certainly is neither limited to nor perpetrated exclusively by financial institutions. Most marketers know the influential power that the interest rate has on the consumer.

When we consumers have our hearts and minds set on a certain car, boat, RV, or other consumer product, if that item is offered at 0% interest, we are the first in line to finance those items over time. Next time you are struck with the finance fever, however, take out a pencil and figure out the *Payment Performance Ratio* (PPR), which is:

> **The Price (or Balance) divided by the payment = the *result*-to-1 ratio.**

In the case of the 19.99% credit card, it had a 180-to-1 ratio, wherein the 6% car had an 18-to-1 ratio. The smaller the number: the worse the loan, because it is eating up more of your cash. This is crucial for those looking to get out of debt as it requires that cash to get out of debt.

More often than not, the 0% interest offers will produce a very low PPR. This is because the 0% interest is normally offered only on new cars fresh off the lot, at the highest possible retail price, over a small period of time (normally 48 months), rather than the 60-, 72-, or 84-month periods. You will find that 0% interest loans create 10-to-1 ratios or lower, eating up huge portions of your cash. The higher the ratio, the better the debt. For example, many HELOCs will have ratios of 150/1 and even upwards of 300/1 ratios during the 2008 recession.

In the grand scheme of things, what 0% interest loans do is consume all of your discretionary income, not allowing you to employ any debt-reduction strategies, which normally require discretionary income.

Don't let the 0% interest-rate temptation snare you into eating up your discretionary income if you are looking to get out of debt. Often, this 0%-interest snare is the tipping point in disqualifying an individual for our program. Set up the accelerated mortgage program first, and then use the concepts and strategies therein to purchase and pay down those purchases.

HELOC Interest vs. Mortgage Interest

Since this new system most often uses the HELOC to accelerate the buy down of the 1st mortgage, it must be noted that HELOCs usually carry a higher interest rate than 1st mortgages in non-recessive economies. Moreover, now that we are employing the use of personal lines of credit, business lines of credit, or other effective lines of credit, these lines always carry higher rates of interest than most mortgages in both recessive and non-recessive economies.

Why are HELOCS often offered at a higher interest rate? First of all, HELOCs are considered 2nd mortgages. 1st and 2nd mortgages are aptly named 1st and 2nd mortgages because of the position (or priority) they hold.

If a consumer defaults on his/her mortgage, the home is put into foreclosure and the sales proceeds are first applied against the 1st mortgage. Any residual proceeds are then applied to the 2nd mortgage.

Hence, a 2nd mortgage (including HELOCs) normally carries a higher interest rate because they carry more risk. It is on this premise that so many CPAs come to me with the following perplexity:

> *Why would you use a 2nd mortgage (or HELOC), which has a higher interest rate, to pay down my lower interest rate mortgage?*

In a nutshell, the title of this chapter answers it: Interest Rates (for the most part) Don't Matter. More precisely, it is because we use small increments of the HELOC and apply those small increments of cash against the 1st mortgage—and then we can more easily pay off these small increments quickly, in repetitive cycles. As our paychecks come in regularly to sit against the small increment of the HELOC loan, the effectual rate (or the actual interest) we are paying on that HELOC is very minimal.

In fact, the cumulative cost of the HELOC over the life of the program (until your mortgage is paid off) is extremely small.

For example, paying off a 5% mortgage with an 8% HELOC within the client average of 9 years will only rack up approximately $3000 in interest in the HELOC.

At this point in my usual presentation to clients, I delve into the math engine and state, "I don't care if the economy fails tomorrow and the interest rate in the HELOC jumps to 18%." Upon entering the increased interest rate (of 18%) into the proper field of the math engine, the pay-off period of the mortgage is pushed back anywhere from 4 to 9 months, increasing the cumulative HELOC interest payments (for the average client's 9-year payoff) from $3,000 to about $5,000.

Bottom Line: If the interest rate of the HELOC jumps from 8.25% to 18%, the mortgage interest savings is slightly reduced from $164,000 down to about $157,000 because the house payments would extend out another 4 months. This is with an 18% interest-rate HELOC—a worst-case scenario.

Although the interest rates for the majority of HELOCs being offered in the 2008 recessive period are lower than the interest rate of most mortgages, it really doesn't matter. The mortgage acceleration concept will produce efficiently with any revolving line of credit wherein the interest rate is under 25% APR.

Chapter 5: Interest Rates (For the Most Part) Do Not Matter

Chapter 6: FAQs of Mortgage Acceleration

In summing up the Mortgage Acceleration concept, I thought it would be worthwhile to list some of the most frequently asked questions posed by my clients and prospective clients.

This whole concept seems too good to be true. Why haven't I heard about this until now?

If you don't want an elephant wandering off, you chain his foot to a stake in the ground. After a period of time and unsuccessful yanking at the chain by the elephant, you can remove the chain, replace it with a small cord, and the elephant stays in place because when he feels the slightest resistance, he stops trying.

We have all *stayed put* for a century or so, despite the removal of the chain.

Moreover, despite the structure of the changing economies, we have been conditioned to stay within the realm of our checking and savings accounts, relics from the Gold Standard.

The only *too-good-to-be-true* aspect of this is that we are finally seeing the errors of our ways after decades of complaining about how unfair banks and other lending institutions are. Perhaps the *too-good-to-be-true* phenomenon arises from the fact that we can stop complaining about the unfair banks, as we now have a choice.

Why would I live out of a debt account while using a credit card to pay for living expenses? This seems quite dangerous to me, and appears to be radical, not conservative.

I don't suppose it was a popular or well-understood idea when the U.S. Forest Service instigated the practice of starting smaller fires (or back burning) in order to fight the larger, main fire (ergo, the phrase *fighting fire with fire*).

Employing the use of smaller portions of the HELOC (good, efficient debt with a 200+/1 PPR) against consumer debt (which is normally inefficient debt); and then apply them against the mortgage will save tens of thousands (if not hundreds of thousands) of dollars in mortgage interest.

With very few exceptions, the interest rate of the HELOC is irrelevant. The structuring of the *cycled transfer amounts* against the 1st mortgage is paramount.

It may help to understand that we are only transitioning debt from one vehicle to another. If we create a $5,000 debt in the HELOC, that same $5,000 is transferred over to the mortgage, reducing that debt by $5,000. Though we still have the same debt, it is transitioned into a more efficient debt account. We can now apply our entire paycheck against the HELOC's new debt for 20 days (or so), and then draw that money back out as we need it and more importantly when we need it to pay for living expenses.

Therefore, our entire paycheck reduces our debt for up to 2/3rds of the month, which shields us from a large portion of the daily calculated interest charged to us in the HELOC, which as I have said many times, creates a type of *reverse compound interest.*

The credit card is only used to pay our living expenses (interest free), keeping the HELOC balance as low as possible, until the credit card is due. The credit card enables us to leverage debt at

0% interest for up to 55 days on most credit cards (when you combine the billing cycle with the interest-free grace period).

Why don't I just put extra cash in a savings account and after it builds up substantially, I will move it against the mortgage?

You can do this, but you won't pay off the mortgage as fast nor save as much interest. By putting the money into a savings account enables the bank to take approximately 96 cents of each dollar, and apply it against their debt, saving them on their accruing daily calculated interest. By taking a healthy chunk of money from the line of credit and applying it against your debt, and then allowing your entire paycheck to sit against that line of credit balance (until you need to start drawing on it for living expenses) is a much more efficient way of battling daily calculated interest. The line of credit structure enables you to leverage your entire paycheck against daily calculated interest until you need it.

Additionally, having access to a line of credit carries the other many offensive and defensive aspects as covered in these first five chapters. Most importantly, the line-of-credit methodology is one of the best safeguards against foreclosure. (Chapter 1)

Will it require discipline to stay on the program?

This answer is a resounding *no*, because this system simply changes *how* you carry out your daily banking practices. Once my clients begin living the concepts, and they see how their paychecks are working against their debt, they find themselves getting enthusiastically caught up in working down that HELOC balance each cycle. The sooner they get the small balance paid off in the HELOC, the sooner they start another cycle: First against consumer debt, then against the mortgage debt. If you are self employed, we use the system to pay off commercial mortgages and business debt.

Most clients only have 15 to 25 cycles to complete, which will span over a 6- to 9-year period before their homes are paid off. Again, *behavior modification* is produced by enthusiasm, not by discipline. And, it most often comes naturally and effortlessly.

What price should I expect to pay for this program?

The market price for the mortgage acceleration service currently runs in the $3,000 to $4,000 range. This price is for various services, or for various lengths of the service, depending on the provider. This price range should include a lifetime of configurations for up to three properties at one time, and should involve licensed financial professionals and/or CPAs who are willing to put their credibility and licenses on the line in backing up their numbers and projections.

At the publishing of this book's most updated version, the mortgage acceleration service has been merged into the nation's most efficient employee benefits package and administered by CPAs at no cost to the employee or employer.

Why can't I just do this on my own?

Many of my clients have come to me after attempting to do the accelerated mortgage program on their own by purchasing a $300 do-it-yourself "math engine". I have also had many clients come to me and pay for my services after paying $3,800 to the multi-level marketing provider, simply because they didn't have the support they needed, nor were they getting their financial answers or the education they thought they had paid for. A mortgage acceleration provider should include the expertise of financial professionals like CPAs and CFPs.

PART II: RETIREMENT FINANCE MODELING

Chapter 7: Deferred *Income* Account (DIA)

I Was Wrong (For Forty Years?)

On October 23, 2008, shortly after the sudden downturn of the market, Alan Greenspan (the architect of our economy for the past 40 years) appeared before a congressional committee to address the causes of the economic collapse. This was on the heels of his personal involvement in blackballing a whistleblower over the OTC derivatives debacle.

PBS Frontline ran the story entitled *The Warning*. The following are excerpts from that program:

RON SUSKIND: You see Greenspan at the hearing table after the collapse, and you see a crushed man, really.

ROGER LOWENSTEIN: He said that the premise that you could trust the markets to regulate themselves was misplaced.

Rep. HENRY WAXMAN (D), California: You have been a staunch advocate for letting markets regulate themselves. And my question for you is simple. Were you wrong?

ALAN GREENSPAN: Yes. I found a flaw, but I've been very distressed by that fact.

Rep. HENRY WAXMAN: You found a flaw in the reality?

ALAN GREENSPAN: Flaw, flaw in the model that I perceived is the critical functioning structure that defines how the world works, so to speak.

Rep. HENRY WAXMAN: In other words, you found that your view of the world, your ideology, was not right?

ALAN GREENSPAN: Precisely. No, that's precisely the reason I was shocked because I've been going for 40 years or more with very considerable evidence that it was working exceptionally well.

JOSEPH STIGLITZ: After almost two decades of public service, he realizes that the economic philosophy that he had pushed so hard, resisting regulation of derivatives, he realized that there were some fundamental flaws in that whole philosophy.

JOE NOCERA: It was a pretty incredible moment that after a lifetime of faith in a certain way the world worked, that Greenspan would say, "I was wrong."

The entire political/governmental/Wall Street establishment has been based upon the philosophies of Greenspan for 40 years: During that same period of time the qualified programs (such as the 401k) were implemented. The 401k as well as the SEP, IRA, 403b, and other similar accounts have proven to be inefficient retirement vehicles and tax traps at best. Americans have lost trillions of retirement dollars and net worth from this flawed structure.

The 2012 Fed Report on Net Worth

In June of 2012, the Federal Reserve released a report on the rise and fall of the average net worth in America. In 1992, America's average net worth was $77,000. Fifteen years later in 2008, America's average net worth rose to $126,000 (an increase of $49,000). In just three short years (2010), the Fed reported that the average net worth was, once again, $77,000. What took 15 years to build was wiped out in just three years.

So, why are we continuing to throw our retirement dollars into losing propositions and tax traps? Moreover, how do we go about finding, qualifying, and establishing a more efficient interest-generating account? These are just two of the questions that the tax-free Deferred Income Account addresses.

Mortgage Elimination: First Piece of the Retirement Puzzle

When the subject of retirement is raised with my clients or prospective clients, the first consideration for retirement is to have their homes paid off. The majority of financially conservative Americans look at their retirement in the same manner; *the first step to retirement is to own their homes free and clear.* Remember, under the accelerated mortgage program, the average mortgage is paid off in 9 years creating an average savings of $164,000 in interest. If the matching employer funds were able to be funneled to mortgage acceleration FIRST (wherein the employers can still create the same tax write offs they get for investing the funds in the stock market), the return on investment for an individual would create a monthly savings of approximately $1,500:

> **$164,000 savings divided by 107 months (average time to pay off home) = $1,532.71/month**

After the mortgage is paid off (in the average of 9 short years), we have an entire mortgage payment (or a good portion thereof) that can be directed toward a safe, sound retirement.

A few exceptions to this rule of waiting until *after* the mortgage is paid off to start retirement funding arise when taking into consideration your *age* and the *amount you have already set aside for retirement*, and especially *where* that retirement is set aside. If you are close to retirement with little-to-no funds set aside for retirement, you may not want to accelerate the mortgage as rapidly, but instead, put more emphasis on the retirement account.

For example, let's say you are 50 years old with no retirement, and we can accelerate the pay-off of your mortgage down to 9 years. A viable strategy may be to push the acceleration of the home back to a 10-year or even a 15-year payoff (so that the home will be paid off by the time you retire), therefore allowing you to apply more funds to retirement.

Now, let's return back to the retirement vehicle itself.

What if there was a financial vehicle that met the following criteria:

- ✓ The fund growth is based on an index that has experienced an average growth of 7.6% over the past 50 years.
- ✓ The fund is not subject to market loss, but instead has a guaranteed gain, or, at minimum, is guaranteed to hold its value when the market goes down; and then participates in the growth once it rebounds.
- ✓ The fund grows tax-free and is disbursed tax-free, with no early withdrawal penalties (if and when the account is configured properly).
- ✓ The fund is not subject to garnishment or lawsuit.

Would such a vehicle not remedy these deep losses experienced in the era of terrorist attacks and of corporate and/or government corruption? It does sound too good to be true, but such a vehicle really exists, and its basic core concept has been in existence for the past 40 years in the form of investment-grade insurance.

Though this seems too good to be true, I invite you to bring your *trusted* CPA or *trusted* financial planner to a seminar so that they can perform the due diligence for you. I always invite such professionals to bring other retirement vehicles to the table so that we can perform an apples-to-apples comparison for productivity as well as for stability, surety, and security.

The Current State of American Retirement

When two planes hit two buildings in New York City on September 11, 2001, retirement accounts lost nearly half of their value. The Arthur Anderson/Enron scandal exacerbated the downturn through 2003, where after the market struggled for the next five years.

Short of making a full recovery to the 1999 levels, in 2007/2008 we experienced yet another massive recession/near-depression, creating another 45% loss in those retirement accounts. Taking into consideration the years required for a full rebound simply <u>to those 1999 levels</u>, when all is said and done, we will have lost a minimum of 16 years of the average 45-year investment window. That is over one-third of the time we have to put away sufficient funds for retirement. Keep in mind that the massive government bailouts will increase taxes to levels never before experienced. Why not pull the funds out now and pay the lower taxes on those funds? Answer: Because of an inhibitor called the Pre-59½ Early Withdrawal Penalty.

For those of you that have been sitting on the sidelines of this conversation finding peace of mind in the fact that your pensions are not subject to market loss, both *government ineptness* or *corporate corruption* (depending on who is managing your pension) are your greatest fears. As reported in Time Magazine (Oct 2005), entire states like Illinois, or cities like San Diego were so far behind on pension payments that *current payments due* to their pensioners were equal to their entire yearly budgets. These two entities were joined by hundreds of municipalities in this 2008 recession. As you will see shortly, two of the largest pensions in the nation are in dire straits.

In the last decade, corporations have sought through court order, to stop paying pensions to avoid going out of business. This is not a tough decision for the courts. If the company in question is forced to go out of business because it can't pay its pensioners, it would result in increased unemployment rates, families going hungry, and thereby adding to the failing economy. Therefore, who should take the hit of a failing company, the pensioners or the current employees? (The *newly-weds* or the *nearly-deads*) To simplify the solution, the courts have two choices, 1) Force the company out of business to safeguard the pension fund (saving the retirees), or 2) let the company default on the pensions to stay in business (saving the younger families). If your pension is in an airline company, sorry, but according to prevalent court decisions, the pensions get cut first.

Ninety-five percent of us are simply relying on our 401Ks or pensions to supplement Social Security. When you see what's left of a 401k after taxes are deducted, and how quickly the fund is diminished when you draw off your living expenses—and most importantly, how quickly the funds diminish in a downturn cycle of the stock market—it is sobering, and even scary.

For government pensioners, remember that many government agencies invest their pension funds into companies in the private sector (such as Enron). When Enron went under, many government pensions took a big hit, or were gutted.

For decades California's state pension funds (CalPERS and CalSTRS) have enjoyed notable success in light of all of the downturns. For years, I have questioned the rave reviews of these funds, baffled at how well they seem to be doing despite all the financial gloom and doom worldwide. Why isn't everyone else copying their model? My skepticism was recently answered: In 2010, the California State Controller's Office released the current condition of these funds:

CalSTRS—Underfunded from $40B to $141B
CalPERS—Underfunded from $35B to $185B

The lower amounts are what the state controller admits as the *Unfunded Liability,* while the higher amounts comprise the *Liability with Market Value of Investments.* To put these numbers in perspective, California's entire state budget for 2009/2010 was $89.5B, which means that just the pension payments for California state workers and teachers (combined) are under funded by as much as one year's total budget for the entire state, and could be underfunded by as much as four years of the state's entire operating budget. This means the state can either continue to pay for law enforcement, infrastructure, fighting wildfires, the current state's workforce (including teachers) and myriad other services, or it can pay pensions. There is not enough money to pay both.

I highly recommend you face your retirement reality as soon as possible, not putting false hopes in your pension, 401k, or IRA if you expect a solid, reliable, stable future and a stress-free lifestyle throughout retirement.

Again, when you realistically look at what taxes alone will do to a tax-deferred or government-qualified account like an IRA or 401k, coupled with market downturns, you will immediately gain a greater appreciation for sound, commonsense retirement planning in the non-taxable environment. Similar to the new commonsense approach of paying off your mortgage in 1/3rd the time (or less) you can now also fund a tax-free, no-market loss retirement in 1/3rd the time (or less).

To sum up this section, you only have to call to mind the advice given by any stock broker who is about to invest your money on the stock market; These professionals will warn you, 1) Don't invest in the stock market unless you can stand to lose it; and 2) If you are going to invest in the stock market, you must be in it for the long term.

Ergo, if you cannot stand to lose your retirement, it should not be in a 401(k), IRA (including the ROTH), or anything subject to market loss. And, the *long-term* investment philosophy should disqualify anyone older than age 40 from having a retirement fund on the stock market at all. Again, retirees don't have *long-term*—they have no room for *any* loss, regardless of the rebound. Moreover, *long-term* and *rebounding* contain *no* redeeming value in the context of retirement in light of the fact that we just lost 16 years of our 45-year investment window. If you lose 50% of your retirement in one recession, you must then make 100% on that money throughout the rebound just to make it back to where you were before the loss. In real terms, this means that you must double your money, for which any stable market index requires an average of 9 years to double your money. This *long-term* caveat alone disqualifies the stock market as a viable method for retirement purposes. It doesn't get any clearer than this.

> [Side Bar: Unfairly, the employees whose retirement dollars are being invested on the stock market do not receive the same warnings as do investors putting their money in the stock market. They are not told that *you must be able to stand to lose it*, or that *you must be in this for the long term.*]

Why, then, do we continue contributing to this losing prospect of retirement investment? Because of the government efforts to *dangle the pre-tax carrot* in front of us, we believe that the *pre-tax contribution* concept saves so much money. In reality, it only creates the incentive to remain invested in a losing prospect.

Pre-Tax vs. Post-Tax Contributions: The Seed vs. The Harvest

To efficiently cut to the heart of the pre-tax contribution issue, I like to use a simple metaphor, followed by a simple question:

Let's say that you are a farmer sitting on a sack of seed, and I am the IRS. I approach you with a tax option: Mr. or Mrs. Farmer, you have the option to pay taxes on either the *front end* or on the *back end* of this transaction. You can either pay me taxes on that sack of seed on which you are sitting, or I will allow you to forego paying me the taxes now (on the seed) if you take that seed, plant it, grow it, nurture it, harvest it, and store it away over the next 30 years, and then I will come back and tax you on the entire harvest.

Which would you prefer? To pay your tax only on the seed (as you receive that seed) where after the entire harvest is tax-exempt; or, to pay your tax down the road on *both* the seed and the entire harvest.

Overwhelmingly, everyone to whom I have ever presented this scenario opts to pay taxes on the smaller seed upfront, rather than on the accumulative seed and the greater harvest in their retirement.

For those of you who struggle assimilating metaphors into real-life application, I just laid out the overall structure of the 401k/IRA/403b/SEP landscape. Our retirement contributions come out of our paychecks *pre-tax*, meaning we don't have to pay taxes on the small increments of money (the seed) coming out of our paychecks to fund our retirement. Instead, you plant that small tax-free seed, nourish it, pay for the fertilizer (and we pay for the "administrator" fertilizer, which often amounts to dung, as this 1.5% *admin fee* is paid to the administrator whether our crop grows or dies). And, over the next 25 to 30 years, whether or not the harvest was productive, we are taxed on *everything*—seed and harvest.

Let's compare actual numbers. If you were contributing $200 per month *pre-tax* into a 401k based on the S&P 500 and you were in the 25% tax bracket, this $2,400 pre-tax contribution over the year decreases your taxable income by $2,400 and *may* put you into a slightly lower tax bracket. To put this in real terms (removing any plausible tax write-offs), if you made $30,000 in one year, and you are in a 20% tax bracket, your tax liability would be $6,000. However, if you were paid $2,400 of that $30,000 through a pre-tax structure, your taxable income would drop to $27,600. Being in the same 20% tax bracket, your tax liability now becomes $5,520 (rather than $6,000). Therefore, over the course of the year, you will have saved $480 by employing the use of the pre-tax contribution vehicle.

However, though you may save those taxes now, you will have to pay those taxes when you start pulling your money out in retirement. It has been Mr. Greenspan's premise that your taxes will be lower in your retirement years because you will no longer be working. In my opinion, Mr. Greenspan did not project for $780 billion tax-payer bailouts of our financial institutions adding to our $15 trillion deficit that MUST BE PAID AT SOME POINT BY THE TAX PAYER; nor did he account for worker-to-retiree ratio declining from 16 workers per retiree, to 2 workers per retiree in the next 15 years. I don't assume he took into account the fact that Americans are living longer either. And, though you don't have a choice whether or not to participate in social security, you do have a choice in which retirement vehicle you will participate.

As I have stated time and time again, *A safe, sound retirement vehicle must be removed from two things: Taxes and market loss.* And, *there is only one vehicle on the planet that carries these two provisional safeguards—a gutted, stripped-down, investment-grade life insurance policy.*

From 1997 to 2010, the S&P 500 index (one of the most stable indexes) averaged a 4.08% annual gain (measured on December 31 of each year). However, because of the major losses and rebound from the two recessions during this period, your money only netted .498% (less than ½ of 1%). (I explain the reasons for this in my seminars.) This .498% is also net of a 1.5% industry standard Third Party Administration (TPA) fee. Therefore, if you had $100K in your 401k in 1997, based on actual S&P 500 results, your $100K gained a total of $6,479 at the end of 2010. Now, because the original $100K was contributed to the 401k in the *pre-tax* structure, your total of $106,479 is now taxed (upon disbursement). In reality, this $106,479 is only worth $85,183 20 (in a 20% tax bracket). That is a difference of $21,295.80. If your pre-tax savings were $480/year (in the example above), the price you just paid is 44 times that yearly savings. But, taxes will be much higher than 20% on this money, especially when you take into account the *Pre-59½ Early Withdrawal Penalty* and the age *Age-72 Penalty* (for not pulling enough money out of the account soon enough).

It is for this reason I am endeared to the nomenclature *tax trap*, to describe the government sanctioned, pre-tax, qualified programs. They've got you coming and going. These penalties ensure that you will pull out the most money possible within a certain time frame (post-59½ and age 72), wherein you will be taxed at the highest possible rate. Even the name is misleading. Your contributions "qualify" to participate in something that turns out to be to your least advantage.

Though the prospects of investment-grade insurance may make your hair stand on end, it is the only vehicle currently on the market offering protection from both *taxes* and *market loss*. And though insurance has had its share of downsides (various scams through the years), it would be unwise to throw the baby out with the bathwater. The securities industry clearly has just as many (if not more) downsides, which proved to be much more expansive and devastating. I provide three simple steps to avoid insurance scam, along with an extensive check list. In that I have devised a particular approach to, and formulation of, this specific strain of investment-grade insurance, I have named that entire formulation a *Deferred Income Account*, as opposed to the government's *Deferred Tax Account.* The two concepts are juxtaposed to each other.

To illustrate this, let's say that you contributed $200/month into a 401k riding on the S&P 500 for the past 13 years. With administration fees of 1.5%, you would have earned approximately .5%, one-half of 1%. Your contributions of $31,200 (*basis*) would have grown to $32,229.40 from 1997 to 2010. Yet, if your tax bracket is also 25% when you are ready to pull this money out, the post-tax value is actually $24,172.05.

Comparatively: A Deferred Income Account (DIA) does not qualify for the pre-tax benefit, and given the same tax bracket of

25%, reduces our $200/month contribution down to $150/month. This creates a basis of $23,400 over 13 years. And, while the S&P 500 averaged .5% for funds *directly* tied to the index, the DIA *indirectly* tied to the same index actually averaged 7.63%. However, because there are no-losses in this account, your money actually does better than the 7.63%. (Some accounts actually contain guaranteed gains.) In the case of a 42-year old healthy male policyholder, he averaged 9.72% on the money from 2007 to 2010, resulting in an account value of $46,669.85—completely non-taxable. Now, to compare apples to apples, we have to take out the insurance costs for those 13 years, which was roughly $1,212 per year, for a total of $15,756 for an account value of $30,913.

What is most important to note in this comparison, however, is the fact that on the next market downturn, that 401k (with a value of $24,172) can be cut in half. The $30,913 DIA will retain its value, and will gain with market upturn, and, hold on market downturn. With every market downturn, the disparity or the gap between these two accounts will grow larger and larger, and the 401k will never catch up to, nor be able to compete with, the DIA.

There are many readers who will be ahead of the curve and find satisfaction in the fact that they have already chosen a *post-tax vehicle* like the ROTH IRA, and therefore have already addressed the *seed vs. harvest* issue. I do applaud this pre-tax prowess, but also offer this heads up:

- ✓ Your ROTH funds are still subject to market loss, and therefore, the *Loss & Rebound Cycles.*
- ✓ You have caps regulating how much you can contribute each year into the ROTH, which caps are minuscule.
- ✓ The ROTH is still subject to the Pre-59½ Early Withdrawal Penalty.

These drawbacks can be completely eliminated.

[Side Bar: For my clients who have already engaged in the mortgage acceleration program, their mortgage will be eliminated in an average of 9 years. Once the mortgage payment is eliminated from the budget, we can hyper-fund a no-market-loss, tax-free retirement in just a few years. Hence, we want to avoid any "caps" or funding limits on the contribution, like those that exist with the ROTH.

When structuring your mortgage acceleration, we can simultaneously structure the retirement. To me (and the majority of my clients), eliminating the mortgage is the first half of a sound retirement strategy.]

Moreover, there are those who believe that by moving from a pre-tax vehicle to a post-tax vehicle you would lose your employer's "matching dollars". This is not the case: Employers can contribute whatever they wish to wherever they wish and still enjoy the same deduction (with the exception of the FICA pre-tax contribution, which amounts to about $7 per $1,000 of payroll. For the employer, this would equate to a $350 loss per every $50,000 of payroll). More precisely, employers can contribute whatever levels they wish to different individuals, as under this approach they are removed from the federal mandate of *what you give to one, you must give to all.* This alone will enable the employer to make up for the $350 pre-tax *FICA match* deduction.

Before getting into details of viable retirement strategies, there are many more problematic issues to understand and to overcome in the overall retirement structure. Just as I have discovered flaws in the banking and mortgage finance structures, there are serious flaws in the retirement structure and within the prevalent retirement paradigms.

The Hierarchy of Investment Security

In my hierarchy of retirement security, I will start with the worst vehicles for investment, e.g. those carrying the highest risk and the least profitability. One of the worst investments is the type wherein the investor (an average individual with few investment skills who works fulltime with very little time to babysit his investment) must rely on someone else to invest for him. In other words, the investor who must rely on companies like AIG, Lehman Brothers, Goldman Sachs, Behr Stearns *et al,* who not only mismanaged their clients' funds, but also mismanaged the overall company, requiring our tax dollars to bail them out, one of which is now paying billions of dollars in bonuses (not wages) to their *mis*-managers for their "good work". It is these examples that paint a bleak picture for securities-based retirements. They are both unstable and inept. At the updating of this version of the book, the principals of MF Global cannot account for $1.2 billion of their investor's funds. This does not happen in the life-insurance realm, and, no, you can't claim that it happened to AIG. All of AIG's investment-grade *life insurance* policies were unaffected, as the state of New York highly regulates the life insurance industry, ensuring that life insurance companies selling investment-grade life insurance in their state maintain approximately 110% of the policyholder's account value in reserves. Quite impressive when you consider the fact that banks only have to maintain an average of 6% to 10% of the depositors' account balances on reserve. There are many other safety factors in this industry that do not exist in other industries or investments, which I will cover shortly.

When meeting with my clients, I like to graphically present what I call the *hierarchy of retirement-fund security*, pointing out that we, as Americans, have been conditioned to shove our retirement money into the *canary cage*.

To start this process I ask my clients, "What role did the canaries play in the mining industry during the 1800's and early 1900's?" Answer: Canary cages were strung throughout the mines and when a canary keeled over, the miners got their butts out of the mine, as canaries are very sensitive to oxygen deficiency or the presence of dangerous gases.

Stock Market

In this metaphor, the canary serves as the *indicator* of healthiness (or the danger level) within the mining environment. Likewise, the stock market is the *indicator* of our financial environment. In the case of the 9/11 terrorist attacks, the canary keeled over and nearly died. The cage itself was nearly damaged, having to shut down for a period of time (the first time in history during normal operating hours). And, because our money was in the metaphoric canary cage, so went our retirement funds: They keeled over.

Not only did the accounts keel over, but we couldn't get out of the mine. Uncle Sam was standing at the opening of the mine shaft with his hand extended saying, "If you want out and you are younger than 59½, you must pay me 10% in addition to your normal taxes before you can exit this mine."

This begs the question, "Why are we placing our retirement funds on the volatile *indicator* of the economy?" In the heydays of the late 1990's, depositing our funds in the indicator proved extremely profitable. You could close your eyes, throw a dart at the financial section of the newspaper, and make money on just about any stock it hit. Things were so good that the dart didn't even have to hit the stock market section to make money. In the post-9/11 era, the stock market hasn't done so well, and stock market investing has required stock market savvy rather than just dart-throwing ability. You just can't point, click, invest, and then expect a return on your money.

Retirement dollars should mainly (and perhaps only) be participating in investment vehicles that are continually going in an upward direction and never in the downward direction.

For example: If the S&P 500 has averaged a 7.6% return over the last 50 years, then wouldn't it be just as beneficial to put your money in a similar vehicle that gains the same 7.6% average, but also carries guaranteed gains and no losses? These guaranteed gains would appease those of us who stood around the water cooler a week after 9/11, saying, "I should have taken my money out of the stock market and put it into a savings account. I would have retained all of my earnings" In the stock market, this would only have been feasible with a crystal ball so that you knew when to pull your money out. But even then, the government would have penalized you 10% for pulling it out previous to age 59½--and that is *only* if your employer allows it, as many do not.

In a *Deferred Income* account (as opposed to a *Deferred Tax Account*—like the 401k), you don't need a crystal ball to know when to pull your money out of the stock market and put it into a savings account. In essence, this happens automatically, as the correct insurance product has a protective, guaranteed floor, or stop loss. This means that your money is protected against loss when the stock market goes down. These guaranteed floors have ranged from 0% to 5%, each having its own particular pros and cons.

Back to the basic premise of stock market investing: If you can't afford to lose it, don't invest it. Hence, the vast majority of Americans involved in 401Ks, IRAs, and other market-based vehicles are firmly and readily stating: *I can afford to lose my retirement money.*

For the majority of us, we are not directly involved in the investment process of our 401k or IRA. Our employers usually select a Third Party Administrator (TPA) who selects the general family of funds, at which point you, the employee, can choose how much of your investment you wish to place in an aggressive fund, how much to place in a moderately aggressive fund, and how much goes into a conservative fund. Then, we sit back and wait and hope throughout the years, smile, then frown, smile, frown, smile and frown with each passing peak and valley of the stock market. As we get older, the worry sets in as the peaks and valleys become more intense and the account remains unchanged *over the long-term* of the last 16 years now. This has not been so much of a rollercoaster as it has been a 16-year ride on a merry-go-round. We are ending right where we started, year after year (soon to be *decade after decade*).

A few of us turn to self-directed funds, where we can choose more precisely where and how our funds are invested. However, regardless of whether these self-directed vehicles are IRAs, ROTHs, 401Ks, etc.; they are all subject to market downturn resulting in loss. If you have both the know-how and the time to baby-sit these funds daily, more power to you. Most of us don't.

In my *hierarchy of security*, the least security for retirement dollars is found in the stock market. Let's look at other vehicles that are more stable.

Municipal Bonds

One of the lower-risk, conservative investment choices is municipal bonds. Because they are low-risk, they are normally low or slow growth. Creating municipal bonds is the method by which municipalities raise money for their community projects. They are willing to pay interest on the money you loan them (or invest with them) via these bonds.

Bonds often carry just as many risks as do the private companies listed on the stock market. In my opinion, I would much rather invest in *privately-managed* projects than invest in *government-managed* projects. Either option, however, requires homework and due diligence.

This economy has exposed "the books" of a plethora of municipalities and states. Many have faced bankruptcy. Muni-Bonds just don't have the same safe, conservative warm-n-fuzzy feel to them as they once enjoyed. And, the commitment to tie up your money for such long periods of time simply isn't worth the long-term/slow-growth investment given the new, more realistic retirement parameters.

Moreover, with the 2011 downgrade of the U.S. credit rating along with the rate at which the Fed is buying up U.S. bonds with worthless *paper-note transactions* of its own, U.S. bonds are becoming less and less appealing.

As of 7/23/2012

AAA RATED

ISSUE	Maturity Range	Today	Last Week	Year Ago
National	10 Year	2.00%	2.05%	2.70%
National	20 Year	3.25%	3.45%	4.15%
National	30 Year	3.50%	3.55%	4.40%
Florida	30 Year	3.40%	3.50%	4.35%

AA RATED

ISSUE	Maturity Range	Today	Last Week	Year Ago
National	10 Year	2.35%	2.40%	3.20%
National	20 Year	3.65%	3.75%	4.50%
National	30 Year	4.25%	4.30%	4.95%
Florida	30 Year	4.20%	4.25%	4.90%

A RATED

ISSUE	Maturity Range	Today	Last Week	Year Ago
National	10 Year	3.10%	3.15%	4.20%
National	20 Year	4.25%	4.30%	5.10%
National	30 Year	4.50%	4.90%	5.85%
Florida	30 Year	4.80%	4.85%	5.80%

****These figures will change as this book ages, and bonds may once again be a viable retirement diversification option.**

Banks: Savings and CD Accounts

Often when our stock market-based (401k) funds plunge, we find ourselves making this statement:

> *Had I only pulled my money out of the market and put it into a savings account, I would have come out ahead.*

However, for those of us old enough to remember the Savings & Loan meltdown of the 1980s, the banking option doesn't offer much security either. In the case of the Savings & Loan scandal, it was a simple matter of greedy, unwise bankers who took depositor funds and invested the majority of those dollars into oil and gas projects. To be more precise, they were mostly *speculative* oil and gas projects.

This massive meltdown exposed the FSLIC's (Federal Savings & Loan Insurance Corporation) inability to actually insure the depositors' funds. Upon its failure, the FSLIC was merged with the FDIC (Federal Depositors Insurance Corporation) to enable the government to save face, thus maintaining the confidence factor necessary for banking institutions to operate. Their claim that they can insure depositor's funds of up to $250,000 does not even amount to smoke and mirrors. It is an outright lie. Not even the U.S. government has enough funds to ensure the deposits of all Americans.

Today, many financially conservative Americans put their money in Certificates of Deposit (CDs) at their bank, maintaining the position that although they won't experience the nominal growth of the stock market, at least their money is safe up to $100,000 per individual or $250,000 per couple (or so claims the black and gold sticker adhered to your bank's drive-up window).

Though our money may be substantially safer in the banking institution than in the stock market, a bank is certainly not the safest place for our money.

The FDIC fund (which is used to bail out failed banks) currently has enough funds to cover 1.25% of all deposits of all banks. Therefore, if more than 1.25% of the banks fail, that fund would be depleted quickly, at which point they turn to taxpayers to make up the difference as they did in the 1980s Savings & Loan meltdown. But now (post-2008), the taxpayers (ergo *the Feds*) are out of this kind of *big bail-out money.*

So, what would happen if 25% or 30% of banks fail? Sure, the banks have assets that can be sold if there are buyers for those assets, but neither the FDIC nor the taxpayers have this kind of money.

In reading a recent FDIC blog, a consumer posed a question to the FDIC: *My investment advisor told me that if my bank fails, the FDIC could take up to 99 years to pay my insured deposit accounts...and would only pay 17 cents on the dollar. Is this correct?*

The FDIC responded with this: *In the unlikely event that a bank was to fail, federal law requires the FDIC to pay 100% of the insured deposits, with principal and interest as soon as possible.*

Now for the legalese: *In the unlikely event that a bank was to fail...*

Is the FDIC stating that banks don't fail? That such an event is "unlikely?" Are banking institutions immune to corruption? No. Is the FDIC insinuating that the FSLIC failure and the ensuing requirement that it be merged with the FDIC in order to prop up the confidence of the American depositors didn't happen? Has Congress not been proposing that the current FDIC structure, policies & procedures, funding limits, insurance premium levels all be revised, and that these requirements be imposed upon non-participating banks? For decades, Congress has been considering substantive reforms with landmark legislation for the necessary overhaul of the FDIC; and necessarily so.

Let's address another word in this same sentence: *In the unlikely event that* ***a*** *bank was to fail…*

Forget about *a singular* bank. What about 100 banks failing? What about 1,000 banks failing? Would it then take my FDIC-insured payout down to 17 cents on the dollar? No. It would most likely be 10 cents on the dollar depending on my particular bank.

Here's a confidence builder: *Federal law requires the FDIC to pay 100% of the insured deposits, with principal and interest as soon as possible.*

This is about as hollow as an answer can get. Who makes, amends, and rescinds Federal laws with a snap of a finger? The Fed. With the clause, "as soon as possible", how easy is it to amend this law? Better yet, forget amending it. As it stands, the clause is much more protective for the FDIC if they can pay it back *as soon as possible.* Let me guess who the governing body is that will determine when *as soon as possible* is possible…the FDIC or the Fed? Does it even matter?

Let's address the 17 cents on the dollar: If they don't have to pay you back until *as soon as possible*, then you don't get anything until they deem *when* they can pay you. But, for confidence sake, just know that it will be *as soon as possible.*

This $100,000 "guarantee" ($250,000 for couples) is viable only if a few banks just happen to "simultaneously go under" for some quirky, "simultaneous mismanagement coincidence." This "guarantee" will have no value in any substantial economic meltdown comparable to the depression.

So why is the banking industry able to make such a claim? It is (by government fiat) necessary to create "confidence" within the banking industry. More precisely, it is absolutely essential to establish and maintain *the confidence of the public* in the banking structure. How better to gain that confidence than claim a $100,000 guarantee by the longest standing, most powerful democracy-based government in the world? In reality, this claim is 98.75% hollow (the inverse of the FDIC 1.25% insurance funding level). Keep in mind that (at the printing of this book) banks must only have 6 cents on reserve for every dollar you have on deposit with them.

Relatively speaking, the banking institution is certainly not the safest place to have your money sitting if you are at all concerned about the safety and security of that money.

Other than the risk factor of *losing your money*, the growth is nowhere close to where we need the rate to be in order to create a viable retirement. Also, the miniscule amount of growth that you would realize from putting your money in a savings account (or CD) is then subject to taxes. A bank is simply not an option for effectively amassing retirement funds.

Real Estate

Real Estate is a good retirement strategy depending on many factors. I will often state that it is a *taxable vehicle*. Those employing various real estate strategies will always fire back, "It's not taxable with a 1031 Exchange."

> [Side Bar: A 1031 exchange *only* allows you to <u>exchange</u> or transfer the value of one asset into another similar asset, often called a "like-for-like exchange". Because you are *exchanging* and not actually *selling* the asset, it is not considered a taxable event.]

I then have to counter with, "Yes, but *anytime* you cash in real estate to fund your retirement or to use those funds to pay for living expenses, <u>it is a taxable event</u>." If you hold the properties to create rental income, the rental income is taxable. But, you can't pay your bills or buy groceries with "real estate". At some point when you sell the property or rent the property for retirement income, it becomes taxable. *All* gains from those transactions are taxable. So yes, at the publishing of this book and until tax codes change, real estate <u>is</u> a taxable environment. And, as we have no idea where tax rates will be in 10 years (let alone 30 years from now), you cannot pinpoint how profitable real estate will be for a retirement strategy.

Real estate can create some robust funds quickly given the right environment, purchasing options, and price & values. But, as millions of real estate investors are learning from the 2001 and 2008 economies, real estate certainly has its risks. I love real estate only as a part of a diversified portfolio and not as the means to a *retirement* end—depending on purchasing options. I personally had my fill of being a landlord, and certainly don't want that lifestyle in my golden years, especially when I can make just as much (or more) in a tax-free, no-market loss vehicle that I don't have to baby-sit.

Insurance

Throughout the book, I have alluded to financial "gurus" who have established their *guru-ship* on some pretty risky foundations, such as *never pay your home off*, *get an interest-only mortgage and invest the difference of the lower mortgage payment in the stock market,* or *If you see an insurance salesman coming…run!* (*i.e. avoid insurance*).

While I concur that many insurance salesmen rank right up there with the proverbial used-car salesmen, and most insurance products are a rip-off, *do not throw out the baby with the bathwater.* There is a relatively new insurance product that has surfaced. Since the emergence of this insurance in the retirement realm, I have yet to find any other product that comes close to the productivity and overall safety and stability of this approach.

Until something comes along that out-performs the *Deferred-Income* approach, I continue to recommend it as the safest, securest, and most profitable vehicle of choice for either investment or retirement purposes.

Before getting into the details of this deferred-income approach, let's first address the *security factors* of retirement dollars sitting in *insurance*.

Frankly, though I have come to accept *insurance* as the most secure vehicle, it certainly does not include all insurance types (nor all insurance companies), but rather a specific type of insurance that must be properly configured (I call it "gutted") to enable maximum dollars to flow into it, resulting in tax-free growth and tax-free distribution. Just as important as the *contractually guaranteed* gains offered by these companies is that fact that many of them have been in existence longer than the United States itself, which indicates impeccable management skills.

So, why does insurance rank higher than banks in my hierarchy of security? Answer: Because of a thing called *required reserve ratio*. Since 2005 and up to the printing of this book, banks have been required to have approximately 6% of depositor's funds on hand for cash accounts (checking/savings accounts), and 0% on reserve for time transactions (certificates of deposit).

For the insurance industry, and more particularly, *cash-value life insurance* industry, there are several rating systems, which indicate the financial stability, and more importantly, the ability of an insurance company to pay out claims. In order to earn these ratings, insurance companies are subjected to various audits by rating companies, including Standard & Poor's, A.M. Best, Moody's, and Fitch, to name the largest.

Depending on the specific rating company, their rating system may range from an A++, or an AAA, or an Aaa down to a C or CCC. Higher ratings normally mean a more stable company with the ability to meet its claims, given various factors. However, each rating company's criteria is different.

> [Side Bar: <u>In my opinion only</u>, the rating companies and the systems they have devised mean very little: I would even go as far as to say that some agencies have their

price and they've been on the take. What were the ratings for the five largest investment houses (Merrill Lynch, Lehman Bros., AIG, Goldman Sachs, and Behr Stearns) just days before they collapsed (or nearly collapsed requiring my tax dollars to keep some of them alive) in Black October 2008? Very high A+ or ++ or better. Has there been any fallout or perhaps some backlash from the SEC for these meaningless ratings? None.

I, like Fox News' Gretta Van Susteren, conclude that the failure of these rating companies in 2008 have negated their relevance or usefulness.

These "rating organizations" can (and often do) open the door to extortion if you don't conduct business how *they* want you to conduct your business. Remember that Arthur Anderson was the largest CPA firm that, too, was instituted as a "check and balance" to Wall Street. Yet, this organization betrayed their very trade, and not only cooked the books, but shredded those books in their blatant acts of obstruction of justice. I take ratings, rating companies, government regulatory agencies, and watchdog groups with a grain of salt...if that. Necessary? Yes. Honest and effective? Seldom, and *never* when you really need them to be.]

What is more important is that state insurance departments require that for every dollar of policyholder deposits, insurance companies who sell insurance within their state boundaries must have an average of $1.12 on reserve for every dollar you have in *cash value*. Though this level varies from state to state, this is far and above the requirement levels in the banking industry. The insurance industry is by far one of the most cash-rich and highly regulated industries in the world—far more regulated than banks and investment firms (*evidently*, in the wake of the 2001 and 2008 recessions exacerbated by corrupt Wall Street and blind government (regulatory agencies).

Now that we have identified a safe, cash-robust industry in which to secure our money, we need to identify a financially secure company with 100+ years of management history. You heard me right. We are looking to engage companies that were in existence before the age of the industrial revolution—the point during which (and thereafter) most notable financial events have occurred (*i.e.* economic booms; crashes, recessions and depressions; world wars and world calamities; terrorism, world-economic crises, etc.). More precisely, we are interested in companies that started anywhere from the 1600s to the mid-1800s. As long as they started before the industrial era, they have proven their management expertise.

To create a wish list of safety factors, we first need to identify what could potentially cause a loss when approaching an insurance investment. In its simplest form, the *risk of loss* or a *meltdown* in the banking system comes from mismanagement by the bank's principals, and then an ensuing *rush on the bank* by the depositors (demanding their money all at once). Similarly, insurance companies can have a *rush of policyholders* in the form of too many claims at once.

What could cause a rush of policyholders? Answer: A catastrophe of some type that affects a large portion of that insurance company's policyholders.

Another security factor within the insurance industry is the existence of the National Organization of Life and Health Guarantee Association (NOLHGA), which also monitors the financial status of insurance companies and will act to ensure that companies do not fail the policy holders. Through separate state legislative actions, they have the authority to put a company into receivership or to completely consolidate a company and shuffle its policies and policyholders to other insurance companies (a service that does not exist in other industries in the stock market). Though most states discourage insurance salesmen from using the NOLHGA in the sales process, it adds a crucial level of safety and security to your investment.

The data on their website (http://www.nolhga.com) is extremely informative and shows the checks and balances, the controls, and the cooperation between government and private enterprise to ensure the financial well being of the investors and consumers within the life and health insurance industries.

Playing the Odds

In my live seminars and webinars, I present the concept that investing in our retirement is simply "playing the odds". Any investment is a gamble, and there is no getting around that.

If you plan to retire at age 65, then you must plan on living (and therefore funding your life) until age 95, at minimum. This is 30 years of living expenses without working. Here is a more precise explanation of the financial burden the age-65 retirement expectation places on us: Working from age 20 to age 65 (for non-degreed blue-collared workers (and less than that for fully-degreed workers who often spend much more time in school), we have 45 years to do two things; 1) provide for our families with as good of a lifestyle as we can afford, while 2) simultaneously setting aside funds to allow us to live for 30+ years without working.

In order to accomplish this, it will require some type of investment (beyond that of a savings account that pays 1% to 2%). Hence, we must gamble (*i.e.* invest). Investment, by its very nature, entails risk. To reduce those risks, we must secure the best odds.

Therefore, how do we go about playing the best odds, especially in the insurance realm? Look for a larger insurance company that began in the mid-1800s that has a proven track record for staying in business.

Now that we have the right industry for investment security, and we have identified the best type of company, we now need to identify the most efficient investment vehicle within that company. To remedy America's retirement crisis, a retirement vehicle must be tax-free and completely removed from market loss. Any account that increases income down the road by paying the smaller taxes *now*, I call a *Deferred Income Account*, which is juxtaposed to a *Deferred Tax Account* (401k, IRA, SEP, 403b, etc.)

There are several companies providing this *Deferred Income* structure, some products better than others, and some companies better than others. As I remain the first and longest-running provider implementing mortgage acceleration in conjunction with this *Deferred Income Account* concept, I know how and why this product must be structured in order for it to out-perform all other products on the market. The configuration is not an art, it is a quantifiable science, which is why I prefer to run the administration thereof through CPAs and licensed or certified financial professionals.

Let me re-state my position on this approach: The only reason anyone would use *insurance* to supplement retirement (and many of my clients *use it solely and entirely for retirement*) is because of the *tax-free* provision that this vehicle carries, along with the *no-market loss* provisions. And, even with these provisions in place, the policy must be correctly stripped down so as to perfectly accomplish your needs.

A Brief Life Insurance Overview

There are two general categories of life insurance: *term life* and *cash value.*

Term Life insurance is inexpensive and provides a death benefit for a contracted period of time. Once that period of time has passed, the policy no longer exists, nor does it have any value.

The term life policy is a very useful policy and serves a specific purpose—mainly as a financial bridge to insure that your beneficiaries are able to get from point A to point B in the untimely event of your death, or until your other retirement or investment funds mature substantially to cover any loss.

Cash Value insurance is also known as *investment-grade* insurance. There are currently three general types of *cash value* insurance: Whole Life, Universal Life, and Variable Universal Life (VUL). The basic concept of *cash value* insurance is your insurance premium (what you pay into the policy) is applied in two different directions: One portion goes to pay for the life insurance (or *face value*—the amount your beneficiaries receive in the event of your death), while the other portion goes into the *cash side* of the account, which belongs to you, the policyholder.

Whole Life

Whole Life insurance is really a different beast. Many insurers (and their salesmen) sell Whole Life as a retirement vehicle. From what I have seen and experienced (with the disclaimer that I have not seen every Whole Life product on the market; and many different strains of Whole Life hit the market each year), it should not be sold for this purpose. In those policies I have reviewed for clients, Whole Life is usually slow growth, and the mechanics are counter-productive to a retirement strategy mainly because the premium continues to be paid up to age 100. In addition, from those policies I have seen, the cash benefits are generally structured to be disbursed during your more advanced years (age 80 to 100), and not in the retirement years (age 60 to 80).

For example, I recently analyzed an orthodontist's whole life policy. He is 49 years old and currently in the process of investing $48,000 per year into the policy. By age 65, he will be able to pull out $75,000/year from the policy on which to retire. Yet, he still has to pay the $48,000 premium throughout his retirement. Although he will receive $75,000/year at age 65, his $48,000 per year premium means he only nets $27,000 for the year.

It wasn't until age 82 that his whole life policy caught up to the *Deferred Income* payout. At age 82 on his Whole Life policy, he would be receiving $197,000/year. If he deducts the $48,000 that he would still be paying in the form of premiums (through age 100), he would actually be taking home $149,000 per year beginning at age 82.

In the *Deferred Income Account*, he would cease his $48,000 contributions at age 65. From age 65 through 100, he would receive his $149,000/year in tax-free distributions: 17 years earlier and *in his retirement years*, not in his *convalescing years*.

Variable Universal Life (VUL)

In a nutshell VUL pushers pushed this: *Buy cash value insurance, put the cash side of the insurance policy on the stock market, and while we're at it, refinance your home and put your equity on the market too.* Many firms that pushed this concept also facilitated the refinancing of their client's mortgage.

This concept of the late 1990s crashed and burned when it collided with the 2001 and 2008 recessions resulting in landmark lawsuits. Not only did VUL investors lose their insurance investment (because VULs are tied directly to the stock market), but many also lost the equity of their homes as they were sold on the concept of refinancing their homes and moving that equity into the VUL. Adding insult to injury, when home values fell the policyholder had a mortgage that was much higher than the value of the home.

Universal Life (UL)

Universal Life insurance is one of the more varied or flexible types of cash value insurance. It is under this category of *cash value* insurance that we find the type of policy we use to accomplish our tax-free, no-market-loss investment or retirement account (*i.e.* the *Deferred Income Account*).

Insurance Mechanics and the Blueprint to Avoid Scam

As stated earlier, insurance is one of the most effective, productive and yet conservative vehicles for retirement mainly because it enjoys tax-free status and is removed from market loss, as well as from the federal penalties, regulations, and mandates. However, there are three hurdles to overcome in order to make this vehicle work at peak efficiency; and, unless you can achieve peak efficiency: It isn't worth doing.

Hurdle One—Insurance (Death Benefit)
Remember I just stated that your premium goes in two directions: One portion is applied to the insurance policy's death benefit, while the other portion is deposited into the cash side of the account. The object is to get as much of your premium into the cash side of the account as possible because those funds both grow and are disbursed tax-free, but only when the account is configured properly.

However, the more insurance (or death benefit) you purchase, the smaller the portion of your premium is applied to the cash side or *your* side of the account. Conversely, the least amount of insurance (or death benefit) you purchase, the larger the portion of your premium makes its way into the retirement/investment side of the account.

With this new outlook on (or use of) insurance, we are not necessarily as interested in the "death benefit" as we are in the "life benefit" or better stated, the "investment or retirement benefit". Therefore, we want the least amount of life insurance (or death benefit) possible for the amount of premium we are contributing to the plan.

Hurdle Two—IRS
The IRS knows that whatever money is deposited into the cash-value side of the insurance account will be disbursed tax-free and therefore, through regulations and tax code, the IRS inserts itself into this transaction by stating, "If you put X amount of contributions into this vehicle over a certain period of time, then

you must purchase, at minimum, Y amount of life insurance (or *face value* or *death benefit*)."

It is in this *minimum amount of life insurance* purchased for the maximum contributions in which we are interested. Otherwise stated, we want to pay for the least amount of life insurance so that the maximum amount of our contributions (or premiums) can flow into the cash-value side of the account. Unlike the 401k or IRAs, there are very few IRS regulations at this point, and as long as we abide by them, we can remove all taxation on the growth <u>and</u> distribution of these funds. In fact, these funds are not even required to be reported on your 1040 tax forms. In essence, this account is like the ROTH IRA, paid for with post-tax dollars, however there is no market loss like the ROTH, and *you* decide what the contributions will be (with very few limitations). Unlike the ROTH IRA, this account is removed from the Pre-59½ penalty and other reporting mandates.

Hurdle Three—Insurance Salesmen

The vast majority of scams in the insurance industry occur at the salesman level, which is why insurance salesmen are often held in low regard.

The insurance salesmen's incentive is structured by how much life insurance they sell, NOT by how much makes its way into your side of the policy. As a matter of fact, the salesman makes no commission on any of the funds that go into your side of the account, but only on the amount of death benefit they sell you. Therefore, it benefits the salesmen to either rate you up, or sell you as much life insurance as possible.

Bottom Line: We want to purchase the minimum amount of insurance that the IRS stipulates in order to push the maximum amount of our premium into the cash side of the account. It's that simple. Once those funds are in that account, they enjoy tax-free growth and tax-free distribution, again, with very few limitations.

By clearing these three hurdles, you can avoid most, if not all, insurance scams.

Pros and Cons of the Deferred Income Approach

Before getting into the downside, let's recap all the up-side potential of the Deferred Income Account:

- ✓ Historic growth indexed to that of the stock market without being exposed to stock market loss
- ✓ Post-Tax, Tax-free distribution (seed vs. harvest)
- ✓ No Pre-59½ Early Withdrawal Penalties
- ✓ Account not subject to lawsuit or garnishments
- ✓ The IRS does not set deposit limits on the account "caps" (like a ROTH IRA)

Now for the downside (there are only two):

1) Upon configuring your plan, the contribution parameters must be established up front in the set-up process. Hence, it is not flexible should you wish to contribute *more money* in the future, though there are a few Plan B's for this scenario should you come across additional funds.

   You do, however, have the flexibility to decrease the amount of contributions should you run on financial hardship, and the flexibility to increase the contributions back to the original parameters when you are, once again, financially stable.

2) The account must remain active until the day you die; or better stated, *the account must outlive you* (with the residual death benefit passing to your beneficiaries). I will provide a detailed explanation of this downside later in the chapter.

These two items are not really substantial downsides or "big negatives" vis-à-vis the overwhelming positive aspects that this account provides. Remember that we are interested in the tax-free "life benefit" more than "death benefit". If we need more death benefit, then we simply obtain a cheap term policy to cover you until the Deferred Income Account grows to the level you need it to be.

Example of Configuring the Deferred Income Account

One particular client (45 years old) had no retirement plan and wanted to establish a tax-free Deferred Income Account. Currently, his only retirement asset is a $200,000 401(k).

> [Side Bar: Keep in mind he is going to lose one-quarter to one-third of whatever the 401(k) is worth by age 65 to taxes. Also keep in mind that the 401(k) may not grow at all depending on the future of the economy and/or future terrorist attacks that will have a direct effect on this fund.]

This client has a discretionary income of $1,000/month, which will enable us to pay off his home in 7 years and 5 months under the mortgage acceleration program. However, if he delays starting this retirement fund until his home is paid off, he will be 52 years old rather than 45 years old. Let's say that you (and/or your significant other) need to make an executive decision for this household:

> *Do you start funding your Deferred Income Account at age 45, or do you wait until the mortgage is finished before you start the funding?*

Keep in mind, *time is money* in investment accounts. Also, as this is an insurance vehicle, *age* is a factor: The older you become, the higher the *cost of insurance*. This means that more of the monthly premium would be going to purchase insurance (because you are older), rather than the majority of the monthly premium going to your side of the account.

To arrive at the most cost effective and productive plan for this 45-year old client, we assess the following comparison:

- ✓ How much money will this account produce from age 65 to age 100 if this client funds the account at $600/month from age 45 to age 65?

Compared to:

- ✓ How much money will this account produce from age 65 to age 100 if he funds the account at $1,000/month from age 52 to age 65—so that we can wait until the mortgage is paid off?

Given the fact that he are 45 years old and only has $200,000 in a 401k, and we are able to pay the home off in 7 years and 5 months, we allotted $600 per month of the discretionary income and apply it to the Deferred Income Account. This reduced his discretionary income down to $400, so it will extended his mortgage pay-off date back to 10 years and 7 months. Before becoming my client, the original home pay-off was 26 years and 8 months. He is still way ahead in the mortgage acceleration game.

After 10 years and 7 months, the mortgage is paid off by the time the client is 55 years old, and he will then have an additional $1,400 in discretionary income (income from the mortgage payment that no longer exists) to add to the current $400 discretionary income, taking his discretionary income to $1800.

At this point, he had another executive decision to make: By what amount should we increase the Deferred Income Account contributions? We suggested taking an additional $800, leaving him with $1,000 of discretionary income to enhance his lifestyle, thereby increasing the DIA contributions to $1,400 per month from age 56 to age 65.

Keep in mind that we have the accurate math engine to project when you can conservatively increase contributions (as debts are paid off). These graduated increases must be claimed when we set up the account. If you don't structure the "graduated increases" in the plan during the set-up phase, the additional contributions (over and above the plan) would render the account taxable.

Now, we have one more contribution factor to address: the $200,000 401(k). When you see what *rolling the 401k into the tax-free Deferred Income Account* does in terms of increased distributions after you have passed the Pre-59½ Penalty date, you will most likely want to implement the following strategy:

At age 59½, you can start taking distributions out of the 401k without penalty. So at age 59½ you divide the 401k balance by the number of the remaining funding years (age 59½ to age 65), which is six years, and then transfer that amount of the 401k each year into the tax-free Deferred Income Account. You will have to pay regular income tax on these transfers, but those taxes would have to be paid whenever it was withdrawn, so upon some research of federal and state tax trends, you might as well move it sooner than later. And, by moving the funds from the taxable environment over to the non-taxable environment, the funds will grow and be disbursed tax free from that point forward.

Many of you are probably thinking; *why not just invest the entire $200,000 into the account all at once*? Answer: Such a move would negate the entire strategy of using insurance as a retirement vehicle because depositing large sums of money all at once into a policy moves you into the higher IRS *insurance-purchase* requirement. Therefore, you want to fund the account over a specific period of time (scheduled) so as to not drastically affect that minimum insurance threshold, which event would create a taxable account (becoming a *Modified Endowment Contract* or MEC for the insurance savvy).

An exception to this lump-sum distribution scenario is a *yearly premium contribution* rather than monthly premiums. In the configuration process, you will see how a yearly premium plan will increase your disbursement over a monthly premium plan simply because your money is invested sooner (up front) rather than in smaller parcels throughout the year. But again, you cannot and should not take a large windfall of cash (such as a $100,000 inheritance) and deposit it into this account all at once. The results will negate what you are trying to achieve.

Beware: There is nothing an insurance salesman loves more than someone with $100,000 looking to slam it into insurance. Don't do it. Again, this account must be deliberately configured in a specific manner, scheduled with timed contributions for maximum pay out to you, the consumer—not to the salesman.

Also, if an insurance agent offers to provide you with an insurance illustration (a projection of cash growth and distributions), ask him to run that illustration at a 7.6% growth rate, and not at the typical 11% to 13% as many insurance salesmen do. A 1% increase in the illustrated projection can create millions of dollars more. Indeed, one of <u>the</u> most stable indexes on the planet has created less than 7.6% over the last 50 years.

For example, insurance salesmen often pitched a policy growth rate of 13% in the years of 2004 and 2009 stating, "Last year (in 2003) we did 26%. I am conservatively projecting one-half of those rates." However, in the years preceding these large gains, there were 42% losses. The illustrations should be based on at least a 50-year average of that particular index—not simply based on one or two previous years.

Distributions from the Deferred Income Account

As you will recall from the previous section, I still owe you a detailed explanation of the second of the two downsides to this investment vehicle: *the account must be active until the day you die* (i.e. the account must outlive you). The reasoning for this is because it is a life insurance policy from which you "borrow" money. Ergo, if you close down the account before you die, then you weren't really using it for life insurance, and the IRS will want its cut. As a matter of fact, if you do close the account before you die, all gains (excluding the basis) will be taxed in the year the account was depleted or closed. To illustrate what this means in terms of dollars (and whether you are taxed or not), I will use the example of our 45 year old, with the $200,000 401k.

From age 45 to 56, he contributes $500 per month into the Deferred Income Account, at which point his mortgage is now paid off (through the mortgage acceleration program). Because he no longer has a mortgage payment at age 56, we now have an additional $800/month (approximately ½ of what used to go to his mortgage payment), for a new contribution level of $1,400 toward retirement until age 59½.

At age 59½ he takes his $200,000 401k (projecting for neither loss nor gain over the previous 15 years), pays tax on 25% of the 401k distributions, and schedules a 6-year rollover of those funds into the Deferred Income Account. [However, it must be noted that in this case, that the IRS rates prohibited him from transferring $41,328.72 from the 401k to the tax-free DIA. Therefore, in this particular case, he would live off of the 401k in his first year of retirement, and then begin drawing off the DIA starting in his second year of retirement.

With the given contribution schedule of this 45-year old client, and the added factors that this client is in good health (because this is an insurance-based account), at a 7.6% growth rate, the benefits are as follows:

- ✓ On Day 1, he enjoys the coverage of an $837,456* death benefit. Should he die on the first day of contributions, his beneficiary(s) would receive this money. (Comparing this benefit along with the following tax-free payout schedule to the 401k or any Qualified Pre-Tax account, you quickly deduce that any pre-tax vehicle simply cannot compete.)

- ✓ From age 65 to 100, he would receive an annual tax-free income of $43,823.

The following are the 10-year production benchmarks of his account after age 65 based on his total contributions of $312,871.40 (over 20 years):

Cumulative Distribution at **Year 10** (age 75)
Total Tax-Free Distributions: $438,230 ($43,823 X 10 years)
Residual Death Benefit: $291,081
Total Benefit: $729,311

Cumulative Distribution at **Year 20** (age 85)
Total Tax-Free Distributions: $876,460 ($43,823 X 20 years)
Residual Death Benefit: $248,063
Total Benefit: $1,124,523

Cumulative Distribution at **Year 30** (age 95)
Total Tax-Free Distributions: $1,314,690 ($43,823 X 30 years)
Residual Death Benefit: $412,552
Total Benefit: $1,727,242.

Cumulative Distribution at **Year 35** (age 100)
Total Tax-Free Distributions: $1,533,805 ($43,823 X 30 years)
Residual Death Benefit: $874,356
Total Benefit: $2,408,161.

(As of January 2012 Illustrations)

Costs of Closing the DIA Account Early

Let's say we know that this individual is going to live until age 98, but at age 95, for some quirky reason, he decides to take all the cash value out of the account, thereby terminating the policy. The cash surrender value at age 95 is $1,046,417. Here are the tax implications for closing the account in that year before dying:

Total paid into the policy (called *basis*): $298,980

Tax-Free withdrawals by age 95: $1,372,969 ($45,766 X 30 years)

Cash value of the account withdrawn (closing the account): $1,046,417.

Combined distributions of Yearly Draws ($1,372,969) plus the withdrawal of Cash Value ($1,046,417) equals $2,419,386; minus your contributions or *basis* ($298,980), equals your taxable amount *that year* (at age 95): $2,120,406. With a taxable income of $2,120,406 *that year*, you would be in the 50% tax bracket, which means you would be taxed $1,060,203. In that you withdrew $1,046,417 from the account, and your tax was $1,060,203, you would have to give everything you withdrew from the Cash Value to the IRS, plus an additional $13,786 to fulfill your tax obligation.

Therefore, it really makes no sense to close down the account at that point in life. Remember that if you ever decide to close the account down, you will be taxed *that year* on the amount over and above your basis. As an alternative to this, simply increase your distributions at age 90 to $100,000 rather than the yearly distribution of $45,788. Or, increase your distributions at age 80 to $60,000; it is your prerogative, as long as you don't run out of money, which would terminate the policy.

I hope you can see the massive upside potential of this vehicle compared to your current taxable strategies plagued with market loss.

Deferred Income vs. 401(k) Tied to the S&P 500

Our CPA staff has logged the actual numbers from the S&P 500 in order to illustrate the productivity of the two competing accounts: the *401k* and the *Deferred Income Account*, both being fully funded on day one with $100,000 in 1997. It must be noted that the 401k is subject to market loss, while the Deferred Income Account is not subject to any loss whenever the S&P 500 loses. The results are as follows:

Year	Actual S&P Index	DIA Production	401(k)*	Deferred Income**
1998	26.7%	14%	$128,569	$112,892
1999	19.5%	14%	$153,673	$127,598

Year	Actual S&P Index	DIA Production	401(k)*	Deferred Income**
2000	-10.1%	0%	$138,092	$126,510
2001	-13%	0%	$111,366	$125,434
2002	-23.4%	0%	$ 84,064	$124,371
2003	26.4%	14%	$104,646	$140,734
2004	9%	9%	$112,347	$152,351
2005	3%	3%	$113,983	$156,893
2006	13.6%	13.6%	$127,564	$177,080
2007	3.5%	3.5%	$130,086	$182,075
2008	-38.5%	0%	$ 78,821	$180,727
2009	23.5%	14.75%	$ 95,848	$205,964
2010	12.8%	13.53%	$106,479	$232,396
2011	.003%	0.753%	$131,536	$232,699
2012	13.41%	14.16%	$149,169	$264,250

*Net of 1.2% Admin fees.
**Fully paid-up insurance (for apples-to-apples comparison to the fully funded 401K, net of $1,212 Insurance costs/fees for a 42-year old male, premium health category.

The following are the key *points of interest* regarding the Deferred Income Account in this table:

- There is never any loss. When the S&P 500 goes down, the policy holder is guaranteed from loss. The decrease in dollars is the deduction for the *cost of insurance* (the death benefit).
- In this specific policy, there is an annual ceiling of 14%, with a bonus of .75% (over and above the selected index) each year after 10 years.
- In years 2004, 2005, and 2006 where the *percentage* gain is equal, it must be noted that these percentage gains are based on the dollar value from the previous year. With that said, in year 2004 the 401(k) percentage of 9% is based on the previous year's balance of $104,646, whereas the Deferred Income Account's 9% is based on the previous year's balance of $140,734, and so on for each year. The 401(k) will never catch up to the DI Account. Even more notable is that when the stock

market dives again, the disparity between these two accounts becomes even larger.

- For 4 years out of the 13-year span, the Deferred Income Account maintained its balance (no loss, like the 401k). This illustrates the power of having your money in an account that is always going upward or maintaining—but never downward and then having to rebound, or having to *make up for lost ground.*
- In 2012, the Deferred Income Account had a value of $264,250, while the 401k has a value of $149,169.
- None of the $264,250 in the Deferred Income Account is taxable, while the entire 401k balance of $149,169 is fully taxable. If you are in the 25% tax bracket, the actual 401k value is $119,335.
- The most damning aspect to the government "Qualified Program" is that it is responsible for losing 18 years of investment time because of something I call the *Loss and Rebound Cycle.*

Loss & Rebound Cycle

If you were to ask an investment broker where to invest your money, and he advised you to place your money on the S&P 500, more often than not that stock broker (and most financial planners) will say, "If you put it on the S&P 500, you're going to do about 7.6% on your money, because that's what this index has averaged over the past 50 years. However, this is not true. Though the *index* has averaged 7.6%, *your money* does not average what the index averages because of what I call the *Loss & Rebound Cycle*. Here is how it works:

If you had $100,000 on the S&P 500 in 2000, and in 2001 it dropped 50% (in the 9/11 aftermath), your account would now be valued at $50,000. To make it back to $100,000 would require doubling your money—or making 100% on your $50,000.

In basic finance principles, we use the Rule of 72s to figure out how many years it will take to double your money. To do this, we divide 72 by the average index percentage. In that the S&P

500 averages 7.6%, we divide 72 by that percentage and conclude that it will take 9 years to double our money at 7.6%. Therefore, beginning the *rebound* in 2003 would mean that we will not make it back to the original level until 2012. However, in 2008 we had yet another recession, which put us further behind, resulting in a minimum of 16 years of lost investment time (over 1/3rd of our investment window).

On the previous table, we achieved a high-water mark of $146,768 in 1999; and twelve years later in 2011, the account value is only $106,479. Greenspan's foundation was *really* flawed.

To further illustrate the fact that the *index average* does not equate to your money averaging that same percentage rate, all you have to do is add up the percentage rates in each column, then see how closely the increase of your actual money mirrors that Actual Percentage rate of your monetary increase:

Avg S&P 500 Annual Percentage (for 13 years):	4.08%
Avg Deferred Income Account Annual Percentage:	7.53%
Actual 401k Annual Monetary Increase:	.50%
Actual DIA Annual Monetary Increase:	9.72%

When your fund is subject to the *Loss & Rebound Cycles,* your money does far less than the actual index percentage.

Opponents to these types of vehicles claim that because you are limited to "a ceiling" (14% in this particular policy, as shown in the table above), the insurance consumers don't make the big gains that those in the Qualified Programs experience. Granted in the 2003 rebound, the 401k gained a whopping 26.4%.

However, that percentage is based on the previous year's balance of $84,064 (a total yearly gain of $22,193). Though the gain of the Deferred Income Account was limited to 14%, it is based on the previous year's balance of $123,730 for a total yearly gain of $17,322, taking us up to a much higher level than where the 401k is.

Pinpoint Financial Planning

While presenting to clients, I have often stated that these financial products (the Mortgage Acceleration calculator and the Deferred Income Account calculators) enable me to excel in accuracy as a financial planner.

With a math engine that can predict when consumer debt will be paid, when the mortgage is paid off, and what the interest savings will be (usually in the hundreds of thousands of dollars), I can now *hyper-fund* a retirement. The pinpoint accuracy comes with the fact that in the Deferred Income Account, I don't have to project for taxes or market loss.

As the overwhelming percentage of all retirement products are taxable and as no one can project for taxes, accurate financial planning is normally impossible.

And even more detrimental to retirement than taxes is *market loss*. The Deferred Income Account, by contract, guarantees against any losses, and the account has averaged 7.6% over the past 50 years; and, during the past 13 years in our compound recessions, the account netted a 9.72% gain. As far as the ability to accurately project for your retirement, these two financial products are unbeatable.

Here is a winning retirement formulation:

<u>$ RETIREMENT</u> = $ <u>INPUT</u> X <u># YEARS</u> X 7.6%

With the accelerated mortgage math engine, we can project how much "input" you can afford in any given year. For instance, if the home is paid off in year nine, freeing up $2,000 per month, then let's take $1,000 of what used to go to the mortgage, and for the next 10 years increase your retirement contribution.

To arrive at our projected amount for retirement, all I have to do is manipulate the *input* amount, or if that factor cannot be manipulated, I will manipulate *the years* in which you will be contributing to the fund (i.e. push for a later retirement). And, sadly for some of my clients, I've had to hold the ol' *Come-to-Jesus* meeting, which goes like this: *O.K., we only have 11 more years to build this fund. You only have $1000/month available to go into the fund, but if we are going to hit the $90,000/year tax-free distribution, which your Social Security distributions will supplement (if SS is still available in 11 years), we are going to need another $600/month to hit that mark.*

To arrive at this necessary amount (to reach your desired $90,000/year), we sit down and put everything on the table from refinancing to relocating to retooling your budget.

With the right tools in hand, and the best products in place, *pinpoint* financial planning is a cakewalk.

Actual Client Cases

In a *post-2008 Recession* client case, the results of the account fared much better than the pre-recession illustrations.

One of my Salt Lake City clients started his Deferred Income Account in 2005. As his contributions were relatively modest compared to most clients, his four-year projected growth (at 7.6%) was illustrated to be at a value of $29,153.00. In running his In-Force Ledger in 2009, his account was valued at $36,128.94—a 20% growth over the original projections during a recession that has cut the vast majority of Americans' retirement accounts in half.

In a more recent case, I have a client who started her DIA four years ago (at age 66). She was initially scheduled to contribute $24,000/year for 10 years, in addition to transitioning $75,000 from other retirement accounts at the rate of $25,000 for the first three years. In essence, for the first three years she would contribute $49,000 ($24,000 from income + $25,000 from her IRAs), and then in the ensuing 7 years she would contribute $24,000. Because the extra $25,000 were contributions she could make based on her own discretion, the insurance company was only billing her for the $24,000. In years 2 and 3 she forgot to include the additional two allotments of $25,000; and because of this, the account was short $50,000 for a 16-month period.

To assess what this oversight would do to the retirement that we had projected for her, we turned to her original policy illustration to see what the balance of the account should be at the end of year four. On that original illustration (run on December 5, 2008 at 1:50pm), it indicated that she was supposed to have a Net Account Value of $146,830. Fearing the worst while anticipating the year-end statement in December 2012, we were pleasantly surprised to see that the Account Value had actually increased to $165,900.46; meaning she was $19,070.46 ahead of projections; <u>again, despite being roughly 16 months late on $50,000 of contributions</u>.

PART III: HEALTH COVERAGE & EMPLOYEE BENEFITS MODELING

Chapter 8: Rethinking Healthcare

To most efficiently arrive at an affordable, cost-effective healthcare end, we must know the course we will be navigating—not just our staff (in your behalf), but you, the paying consumer, must know the state of the industry, its strengths, its weaknesses, its trends, and its politics. This chapter will provide a brief overview.

In the healthcare realm, all that most people "think they need" is a low deductible along with a $25 doctor's office co-pay. And, as long as they get these two items, it is almost irrelevant how high the monthly premium is. After all, since the 1980s employers have been footing the majority of the monthly bill. However, in the post-2001 and 2008 eras, employers have been dropping these plans at alarming rates, leaving individuals to either pick up larger portions, or to fend for themselves and acquire their own insurance.

In 2012, many states are months (and millions of dollars) behind on reimbursing hospitals, doctors, and pharmacists for Medicaid bills, resulting in Medicaid patients being turned away.

If you are relying on (or hoping to be able to rely on) any industry such as healthcare, it is extremely beneficial to know it and know its limitations.

[Side Bar: I was fortunate enough to work with Dr. Marc Micozzi who is one of the four members of the medical *Rat Pack* responsible for integrating alternative medicinal approaches into mainstream medicine (Dr. Micozzi's cohorts were Dr. C. Everett Koop—former U.S. Surgeon General under President Reagan; Dr. Andrew Weil; and, Dr. Deepak Chopra).

For two years, Dr. Micozzi and I traveled back and forth between Utah and Philadelphia (at the Thomas Jefferson Institute of Integrative Medicine and Temple University), working together on several educational projects in the integrative realm.

It is from my exposure to the works of these four trailblazers that I came to learn of the issues behind the failure of our healthcare structure, and the value of the other (less popular) medicinal approaches.]

Diagnosis of the Medical Structure

In the 1990s it was an established fact that the health insurance industry thrived on one simple equation: 80% of the healthy population was paying for 20% of the sickly population. However with the evolution of our diet including more processed foods, soil depletion, over medication, and the ever-increasing sedentary lifestyle of the population, these ratios have been evolving to the point where there is much less disparity between this historic 80% - 20% ratio.

Today the healthcare industry is controlled and run by government, insurance companies, and drug companies. The doctor and patient have the least say in the medical transaction, evidenced by the extremely limited time doctors spend with each patient.

Most Americans don't complain about *who* runs the healthcare system, as long as they have a low deductible and the very popular *$25 doctor's office co-pay*. Many Americans will even defend their healthcare system as *the best in world,* while some will even justify the high premiums because *it is the best in the world.*

Though Americans enjoy the most technologically advanced and successful trauma treatment (typically in the emergency room), we fall far behind other countries in other crucial areas, such as infant mortality rates where we have the 34th highest mortality rate (behind countries like Singapore, the Czech Republic, Cuba—and 30 others).

In the 1990s, I came across a study from the American Medical Association stating that our healthcare system was responsible for approximately 86,000 iatrogenic deaths annually (deaths caused by human and systemic errors, or oversights). I recently came across these new numbers:

Condition	Annual Deaths	Cost
Adverse Drug Reactions [1, 2]	106,000	$12 billion
Medical Error [3]	98,000	$2 billion
Bedsores/Convalescing [4,5]	115,000	$55 billion
Infection/Nosocomial [6,7]	88,000	$5 billion
Malnutrition/Nursing Homes [8]	108,800	
Outpatient Errors [9, 1]	199,000	$77 billion
Unnecessary Procedures [10, 11]	37,136	$122 billion
Surgery-Related [12]	32,000	$9 billion
TOTAL	**783,936**	**$282 billion**

Besides the tragedy of the 783,936 deaths, the $282 billion price tag from iatrogenic deaths has also played a role in the demise of our system, bringing about hundreds of thousands of lawsuits, which results in the driving up the costs of medical malpractice insurance for all categories of providers, which results in driving up the costs of medical services, resulting in ever-increasing insurance premiums.

To avoid these high-cost premiums requires education, an open mind, overhaul, and innovation.

Individual Responsibility is the Only Sure Fix

As presented in previous chapters, to quickly free yourself from the bonds of debt in this highly-evolved economic structure, you must think and act like the bank. To free yourself from reliance on Social Security (because it may not be there when you retire) you will need a Plan B (and C and D for peace of mind). As a very specific form of *life insurance* provides the best security for retirement, and because life insurance is based on the status of your health: your lifestyle and health status is crucial because of a thing called *underwriting*.

Underwriting is the process where a company (typically a health insurance or life insurance firm) considers all of the risk factors surrounding YOU (the insured). These factors and the data surrounding these factors are sorted out, analyzed, and categorized into various charts and tables called *actuarial tables*.

It is these tables that determine how much of a risk you will be to the insurance company. These factors often include age, height, weight; degenerative illnesses you may have or have had, where you live (high pollution levels, high automobile-death rates), what you do for a living (*i.e.* a relatively safe desk job vs. working construction where the rate of injury increases), etc. Actuarial tables can be extensive and exhaustive, thereby rendering *underwriting* a somewhat laborious process.

Typically, if you have health or high-risk issues, you are *rated up*; meaning, the cost of insurance will be higher than someone without the health issues. Either in my insurance-based approach to retirement, or under Obamacare (with regard to the *Nanny State's Taxation Measures*), your health status and lifestyle choices will have a direct impact on your finances in your retirement years. NOW is the time to correct behaviors that are detrimental to your health. As long as Americans continue to consume the 64-ounce cola and three doughnuts for breakfast day-in and day-out, the system will remain broken as healthcare prices will increase to pay for the increasing number of illnesses exacerbated by obesity.

The Health/Retirement Link

If you have health issues, your health insurance premiums will be as much as, if not more than, your mortgage; and as stated, as the Deferred Income Account is insurance based (requiring underwriting), the healthier you are, the lower your insurance rates will be, and the higher your tax-free payout will be.

Politically Speaking: Your health is a completely, all-encompassing, financial issue on both macro- and micro-economic levels. Those pushing nationalized medicine realize this, which is why there is currently a push to regulate salt, saturated fats, the size of soft drinks, fast food, etc. Opponents to these regulations cry, "Nanny State!"; but eventually, someone has to pay for this lifestyle, which is quantifiably pushing diabetes, autism, heart disease, and other degenerative illnesses off the charts. Someone, somewhere, at sometime must pay the proverbial piper! Being a fiscal conservative, I can't complain about junk-food regulations any more than I can complain about high taxation on tobacco products. With this comparison in mind, I certainly won't cry, "Nanny State!" And, wherein we won't let people die for their bad decisions, someone must pay the medical bills—bankruptcies don't even pay the bill! Bills that go unpaid are picked up by all of us in the form of higher medical costs. The political right has offered no solutions to these issues, while the political left seems to be addressing the issues at the root cause. Again, being a fiscal conservative, I can't complain about those who are implementing *root-cause* solutions—at least they are attempting to do something. Non-regulation/Laissez-faire policy just hasn't done it!

Lastly, AVOID the advertising gimmicks of the drug companies, who (like the health insurance industry) have positioned themselves between you and your doctor. When you see the TV commercial of that little fluffy ball dragging across the ground with a frown on his face that pops a pill, and is then able, once again, to bounce up and down enthusiastically as high as the other smiling balls: DO NOT run to your doctor and ask for that drug. You are not a ball, and you (as a human being) were not engineered to bounce up and down.

In the financial realm, when you ask for that drug, although it is illegal for that doctor to make money from that drug company (though they get perks through a newly-revised back-door method) that doctor will have to diagnose you with *some illness* in order to prescribe that drug for you. This diagnosis of *whatever-itis* goes on your medical record, at which point you will have a *ding* on your medical report—no different than a *ding* on your credit report, or a *ding* on your driving record. Eventually, you have to pay for those *dings,* as you are reassessed each year by the insurance company.

Just as our economy has morphed through four evolutions, so has the healthcare industry experienced its own evolution. To thrive, you must evolve with it. Learn and thrive.

Covering Your Risks While Limiting Your Participation

The mortgage acceleration concept becomes a tremendous tool in assisting you along the path to becoming self-insured, or even partially self-insured. The basic concept can be summed up in this simple sentence: *If a $250K mortgage balance can be paid down in under 10 years, then a $10K deductible becomes a drop in the bucket.* In other words, by purchasing a high-deductible plan in place of the Cadillac 80/20 plans with low deductibles, your family can save anywhere from $5,000 to $10,000 per year in health insurance premiums if you don't have a claim. If you do have a $10,000 claim, then that deductible would be paid for through the mortgage acceleration buffer account. If, in this case, your mortgage were slated to be paid off in 9 years, the $10,000 setback for that healthcare issue would then take your mortgage payoff back a year or so to 10 years and 3 months.

However, there are products and systems out there that enable you to make money in the event of an accident or illness, which not only mitigate that high deductible (or pay the cost of that deductible for you), but also make you money (over and above the cost of the deductible).

The most common health insurance policy in the industry is the *80/20 Plan.* The typical health insurance policy of $1400 per month for a family (the current national average) normally carries a $1,000 to $3,000 deductible. This type of policy typically contains a $15 to $25 office visit co-pay, and about the same co-pay for prescription drugs. Under the 80/20 structure, you normally pay 20% after you have satisfied your deductible up to a *maximum-out-of-pocket* amount of anywhere from $3,000 to $6,000.

One alternative to the *80/20 Plan* is a *Major Medical, High Deductible,* or *Catastrophic* policy. A major medical plan traditionally has a very large deductible of about $7,500 to $11,000. This means that you must first pay the entire deductible through the course of the year before the insurance company pays for anything. But, after that deductible is satisfied, the insurance company typically pays 100% (as opposed to just 80% on the 80/20 plan).

Historically, the population has been conditioned (and even frightened) away from these high deductible plans with horror stories of bankruptcy, as Americans have been led to believe that a yearly high-deductible of $10,000 is much more difficult than paying $16,800 per year for an 80/20 plan year in and year out. [$1,400/month (for a family plan) x 12 months = $16,800].

Hence, if we can obtain a Major Medical policy for $170 per month (per family) supplemented with specific riders to cover the costs of the high deductible, saving us $500 to $1,100 per month in premium payments, this would equate to a yearly savings of $6,000 to $13,000. If you have 6 doctor visits at $100 per visit (not covered under a major medical policy) that would come to $600 for the year; consequently (on the lower amount), our savings is now $5,400 for the year. If you go two years without a major medical claim, you will have been able to save $10,800, which (in the larger picture) you could apply to your mortgage via the mortgage acceleration program. When you need those funds, you have access to pull them back out to pay the medical costs or doctor's office visits.

Indemnity Supplementation

The element that makes this strategy so appealing is indemnity insurance policies. These are small, inexpensive, incident-specific policies that supplement your high-deductible plan. When I placed the elements of this puzzle together, it was exciting. When I actually had to rely on the elements of this strategy to cover two accidents, it was even more exciting.

In my case, I was in the process of starting this company, and my family health insurance plan was $800/month for my 80/20 plan. As I was self-funding my company start-up, that $800 was stretching my budget too much, as it was nearly as much as my mortgage. I set out to reduce my health costs, so I began considering the high-deductible approach. I found a plan that contained a $10,000 deductible with a monthly payment of $170—ergo, I was saving $630/month in premiums. If I didn't have any claims during the year, my savings would be $7,560. However, as a father of three, the $10,000 still created a certain level of worry. I them stumbled on the indemnity plan concept.

Indemnity policies are contracts that state, "If you have a certain condition, then we will pay you a specific dollar amount." They do not pay the doctor. They do not pay the hospital. They do not contact your high-deductible insurance carrier and negotiate with them in any way. They pay you directly the amount stated in the contract. I obtained a hospitalization policy, an accident policy, and a major illness policy; all three for the price of $130/month. Adding this amount to my $170/month high-deductible plan, I was now paying $300/month, rather than $800/month. At this point, my monthly savings was $500, or $6,000/year.

Shortly thereafter, my son broke his arm while rollerblading and my daughter broke her wrist while snowboarding. In each case, both the emergency room visit and the follow-up doctor's visits totaled $600 (for each accident). In that my deductible (at the time) was $10,000, I had to pay the entire $600 for each case ($1,200 for the two). I then turned to my indemnity policy which covers accidents. The payout for each incident was $2,500. In summary, I was paid $5,000, after which I had to pay $1,200 in medical expenses. I had a net gain of $3,800, enough to pay my health insurance premiums for the entire year. Since then, I have found a high-deductible/major medical plan for the same $170 monthly premium; however, the deductible was reduced from $10,000 to $7,500.

The coverage of the *major illness* policy is even better. If my family or I were to contract a major illness such as cancer, MS, *etc.*, the *major illness* supplement would pay me one lump sum of $20,000. Keep in mind, my out-of pocket deductible in the major medical policy is now $7,500. So, if the *major illness* policy pays me $20,000, then $7,500 of it can be applied to the deductible, after which <u>everything is paid at 100% by the major medical policy</u>, and I still have $12,500 extra cash to apply against my mortgage. In the following year, I can pull that money back out and pay the deductible for the ensuing year if those cancer treatments continue. All this time, I have been saving $6,000 per year in premiums by migrating from the 80/20 policy to the major medical policy supplanted with the appropriate indemnity policies.

Let's put this into perspective: Instead of paying off your mortgage in 30 years on your current system, you are paying it off in an average of 8 years and 11 months. If you were to have a major medical bill of $10,000, your mortgage payoff would simply be prolonged to 9 years and 10 months—<u>if you don't have the supplemental policies</u>. But, if you do have the major medical insurance <u>with the supplemental indemnity policies in place</u>, chances are you will make money on your medical claims. This approach should put the *major medical* insurance policy back into the health insurance dialogue.

[Side Bar: At the publishing of this book, Obama-care would do away with major medical policies of which I speak. If this becomes the case, then the insurance portion of this health insurance dialogue will evolve, and may even become superfluous. However, in that the average client is saving $164,000 in mortgage interest over an average of 8 years and 11 months (as explained within the mortgage-acceleration chapters), this boost in household income can pay a lot of medical bills or help you to be able to afford more expensive insurance. Even as Obama-care calls for cuts in Medicare along with the eventual increase in insurance premiums (necessary to include another 35 million uninsured on the insurance rolls).]

My staff has become proficient at seeking out the best insurance companies and supplemental indemnity policies, and then customizing an affordable healthcare approach at no cost to you other than the cost of the products.

The mortgage acceleration process not only enables you to become your own bank, but also enables you to formulate your own health insurance strategy, creating substantial savings each year, while providing the safety net should you have large claims.

Wherein 80% of the population (and companies) can reduce their healthcare expenses by one-half, while increasing the benefits, this savings is no longer flowing to the healthcare establishments (providers and insurers), but instead remaining in the pocket of the consumer and/or the company. By rethinking your health choices, behaviors, and health insurance options, it creates a massive redistribution of wealth within this industry segment.

Lastly, even with nationalized healthcare, this strategy (in most cases) is still more affordable for employers despite the $2,000 per/employee, per/year penalty (for non-participation by companies with more than 50 employees). The $2,000 penalty divided by 12 months equals $167/month. A $300 to $400/month family plan with the $167/monthly penalty totals $567. This amount is still less than one-half of the national average for family healthcare policies being paid by corporate America in 2012.

Iatrogenic Death Citations

1. Lazarou J, Pomeranz B, Corey P. Incidence of adverse drug reactions in hospitalized patients. JAMA. 1998;279:1200-1205.
2. Suh DC, Woodall BS, Shin SK, Hermes-De Santis ER. Clinical and economic impact of adverse drug reactions in hospitalized patients. Ann Pharmacother. 2000 Dec;34(12):1373-9.
3. Thomas et al., 2000; Thomas et al., 1999. Institute of Medicine.
4. Xakellis, G.C., R. Frantz and A. Lewis, *Cost of Pressure Ulcer Prevention in Long Term Care*, JAGS, 43 - 5, May 1995.
5. Barczak, C.A., R.I. Barnett, E.J. Childs, L.M. Bosley, "Fourth National Pressure Ulcer Prevalence Survey", Advances in Wound Care, 10- 4, Jul/Aug 1997
6. Weinstein RA. Nosocomial Infection Update. Special Issue.
7. Forth Decennial International Conference on Nosocomial and Healthcare-Associated Infections, Morbidity and Mortality Weekly Report (MMWR), February 25, 2000, Vol. 49, No. 7, p. 138.
8. Greene Burger S, Kayser-Jones J, Prince Bell J. Malnutrition and Dehydration in Nursing Homes: Key Issues in Prevention and Treatment. National Citizens' Coalition for Nursing Home Reform. June 2000. http://www.cmwf.org/programs/elders/burger_mal_386.asp
9. Starfield B. Is US health really the best in the world? JAMA. 2000 Jul 26;284(4):483-5. Starfield B. Deficiencies in US medical care. JAMA. 2000 Nov 1;284(17):2184-5.
10. Calculations detailed in Unnecessary Surgery section, from two sources: (13) http://hcup.ahrq.gov/HCUPnet.asp and (71) US Congressional House Subcommittee Oversight Investigation. Cost and Quality of Health Care: Unnecessary Surgery. Washington, DC: Government Printing Office, 1976`
11. HCUPnet, Healthcare Cost and Utilization Project for the Agency for Healthcare Research and Quality. http://www.ahrq.gov/data/hcup/hcupnet.htm,
12. Agency for Healthcare Research and Quality http://www.ahrq.gov

Chapter 9: Reconfiguring Employee Benefits

In that the 401k is a losing prospect (Chapter 7), and the 401k is the key component to the vast majority of employee benefits packages, it is time to rethink and reconfigure America's employee benefits packages. To this end, I began researching the pros and cons of structuring these services, not simply as an additional employee benefit, but as *the core* of any employee benefits package. Though I will discuss the reason in detail, the overview of reasons is as follows:

- As presented in Chapter 7, security-based retirements and *tax*-deferred accounts are highly inefficient vehicles for retirement: The Deferred Income Account is much more productive and secure.
- The latter offers both the employer and employee much more freedom, being removed from many of the federal mandates and penalties.
- There are no costs to the employer or the employee for these services (outside of what is being contributed to the employee's retirement or to the particular health plan), producing substantial savings for both employer and employee.
- The overall savings of the mortgage acceleration program coupled with the Deferred Income Account (Chapter 7) will put much more money in the hands of the employees, an instant *raise* so to speak.

U.S. Supreme Court Unanimous Ruling

On February 20, 2008, the U.S. Supreme Court unanimously ruled that individual employees can now sue their employer for 401k losses. (LaRue V DeWolff et al.)

Think about this carefully. This is an entirely new field of law that Alan Greenspan's economic structure has created as an unintended consequence. This new liability for employers has the potential to be devastating to business and, therefore, to our economy.

Many legal advisors are advocating that companies revisit and refortify their contracts with their TPAs (Third Party Administrators) and/or those who are managing the funds in their employees' retirement accounts. This, however, severely misses the mark. In the LaRue v. DeWitt (et al.) case, it isn't the TPA that is solely at fault. It is also the HR department employee.

Before this ruling, it required the entire employee group to bring a case against the employer. In that individual employees can now sue an employer, the risk is increased exponentially. As per historic precedence in new legal fields, the *reasons why* an employee can sue for the 401k losses will begin to increase despite the fact that the majority of employers have no expertise or control over the growth or loss in retirement accounts.

On the other side of the coin, the practices of many employers in this realm have run the gamut of *questionable* or *unethical* to both *fraud* and/or *theft.* In many cases, employers are receiving perks, kickbacks, and even making money from the placement of their employees' retirement accounts. This clearly creates a solid conflict of interest.

Historically, employers feel that it is they who should decide who manages the account (be it a family member or close associate) because they are contributing to the account and they are the "authority" over all of the participating employees. However, in most cases it is the employees who are contributing the majority of the money into those accounts. Their involvement in the decision-making process (of who manages the account) should be paramount in light of this new ruling. It is my recommendation that employers completely remove themselves from the equation, and therefore from this new risk entirely. It could be devastating 20 years down that road when the employee no longer works for you, yet shows that because of a "lack of communication" in the HR department, the retirement account should be $300,000 rather than $75,000. From what I have seen, the various statutes of limitation (SOL) in this field are not yet established. When they are established (and/or as the SOLs evolve with landmark cases), I would assume that the judiciary will include such clauses that *the SOL clock starts ticking upon discovery of the act*. If discovery happens 20 years in the future when the ex-employee begins drawing from that fund, the liability can easily put entire companies out of business, as the company would then be responsible for 20 years of fund growth, rather than for the much smaller amount when the mistake occurred.

Again, the easiest, surest, and least expensive resolution to this new liability is to completely sever your company from the risk. Your employees will be extremely happy with the transition when taking into account the individualized health insurance options (Chapter 9), as well as the no-loss, non-taxable retirement approach (Chapter 7).

Rights vs. Benefits

In 1978 when the government stepped into the employee *benefits* arena, the very concept of *employee benefits* evolved into *employee rights*, and that is exactly how individuals perceive *employee benefits.* They are now *rights.*

This perception of *rights vs. benefits* evolved from the implementation of federal mandates legislated throughout the 1970s, which dictate such tenets as *what you give to one, you must give to all.* If the government states that you *must* give the same benefit to all individuals regardless of productivity levels or merit, it is quite easy to understand how *benefits* have evolved into *rights.*

In this employee benefits approach, employers can offer the benefits to as many or as few as they wish, just as they would an executive bonus plan, but much more simplified. This proves to be extremely beneficial for those employers who do not provide a 401k plan because they cannot afford it for *all* employees (as the mandate stipulates), and for employers who have suspended their 401k plans and cannot afford to re-start the program for their employees. Under our plan, employers can extend these benefits to one, five, or one hundred employees at a time; they can bring on one department at a time, or extend the program to those with the most seniority or productivity, or by management levels, or in any manner the employer sees fit.

Although the healthcare benefit is subject to federal mandates for employers with 50 or more employees, our healthcare approach is one-quarter the cost of all other healthcare approaches on the market, and the plans are individually structured according to needs and affordability.

Benefits are now reclaimed as such: *Benefits.*

Re-Educating Corporate America on Benefits

I have come to see that most employers don't realize the extremely grave responsibility they have in making the correct decisions (when it comes to the retirement funds of their employees). Where the employees have more at stake, shouldn't employees be included in the decision-making process? In the vast majority of cases, employees have no say in this decision, but only a say in whether they want their fund to participate in a high-, medium-, or low-risk fund predetermined by the fund manager.

> [Side Bar: More sadly, yet more realistically, I doubt that more than 20% of the employees would come to the due-diligence table if given the invitation, nor would they take it upon themselves to research a fund manager. However, if they did, chances are they would discover the fund manager is a relative or friend of a company principal from whom the company is receiving kickbacks or perks of some type. This, alone, would be worth the employees' inclusion.]

I have come across many companies where the retirement fund of the employees is a revenue center for the employer. This being the case, it creates a conflict of interest. For instance, if the employer is making money off of the employee accounts, why would the employer care *what* the fund actually produces for the employee, just as long as it creates the biggest kickback for the employer?

Regardless of whether the employees' retirement accounts suffer from the employer's poor choices, the employer has historically been removed from any liability. *Employees* should be educated on this predicament and should be given the option to play a more active role in their own retirement. If the employer is involved in the manner described above, the plan, the players and their roles, and the perks or kickbacks being created should be fully disclosed and should inure to the benefit of the employees. It is these types of practices that give rise to unanimous Supreme Court rulings such as LaRue v. DeWolff.

In the wake of our decade-long recession, and in light of the loss of all the retirement dollars from 2001 to the present date, the time is long overdue that employers begin rethinking their behaviors and the crucial role they play in their employees' futures.

And, if they cannot do what is right for each employee in the retirement arena and stand behind their decisions even long after the employee has left their employ, then companies would be much better off getting out of the retirement business. Again, this is (in part) the best resolution.

Employers do not have the time to be fully interested and engaged in the well-being of employees' retirement accounts—especially after those employees have left these companies (in terms of pension accounts). This is a faulty structure void of any accountability (until it is too late, or, with this new U.S. Supreme Court benchmark case, until the employer is sued). This structure has paved the way for corruption, which has historically proven to be to the detriment of the employee.

In most cases, throughout all these years, the employee is led *to believe* that his retirement is being properly managed. Depending on the behaviors and decisions of the employer, it can create an unquestionable theft of investment time. In the financial investment realm, *time IS money.*

> [Side Bar: I hope you can see the fast-forward outcome of this Supreme Court ruling. If even an employee can create this level of quasi-indictment against employers, can you imagine the cases poised to ooze out of the proverbial woodwork when Ivy-Leaguer attorneys gain their stride?
>
> Though I consider myself a free-market leaning conservative (who has an appreciation for the necessary *balanced regulation* and oversight, and one who repudiates *laissez-faire* policy), our current "retirement structure" that has virtually no checks and balances (where the administrator makes money regardless of gains or losses in the investment equation) is well beyond my comfort level, and should be beyond yours as both employers and employees.

> The future financial well-being of individuals cannot be left to "capitalist devices" wherein there are no checks and balances, especially where there is no accountability for retirement account losses. Keep in mind, companies are defaulting left and right on their pension programs, leaving the employees destitute in many cases. Again, this practice literally robs individuals not only of what was contracted to be theirs, but on top of that, robs them of the *time* that they could have/should have been growing their retirement elsewhere.]

To begin solving the retirement dilemma that currently plagues America, corporate officers (including HR personnel) will have to put in the time to research the nature of tax-deferred vehicles and other funds directly tied to the stock market. Again, from Chapter 7, if 95% of Americans feel that *pulling the equity out of their homes and placing it on the stock market* is a bad idea, then (roughly) that same percentage of employers should realize that the stock market is no place for their employees' retirement funds.

I recently came across a case where the company had not only stopped contributing to their employee's 401k plan, but this company also *required* its employees (through undocumented pressure) to continue contributing to their 401k accounts, despite the company discontinuing its matching contributions.

The CFO of this company loved all the concepts I presented to him, found no problem with the approach, and loved the fact that the benefit package included the mortgage acceleration services administrated by CPAs who work individually with each employee at no cost to the employee or the employer. Toward the end of the meeting, this CFO started asking, *What's in it for me*? I repeated all the reasons:

- No taxes
- No market loss, but only guaranteed gains
- No pre-59½ early withdrawal penalties
- Fewer mandates imposed on the employer
- No cost or fees to the employer or employee

- Professional assistance in finance and retirement planning free of charge
- Ongoing financial education to the employers and employees by CPAs at no charge
- A much more affordable approach to health insurance

And, yet, he kept posing the question: *What's in it for me*? It was at that point I realized the extent of the *corporate hand in the employee cookie jar*. Legal? Yes and no. Acceptable? That depends on your ethics. A good idea (in light of the new legal landscape)? Not at all.

The Misperception of the Employer's Tax Write-off

Often when speaking with HR personnel, they are concerned that if they participate in a post-tax vehicle, the employer will lose the matching tax write-off. In other words, they perceive that there is some special tax-incentive for participating in the 401(k) by getting a special *matching* tax incentive if they contribute to the employee's retirement fund.

This is false. Whatever employers pay to employees (whether it is salary or matching retirement contributions or health insurance contributions) <u>reduces the amount of their gross income, thereby reducing their tax liability</u>. More clearly stated, if an employer contributes to an employee's health insurance, this contribution is an *employee expense* that, in turn, reduces employer profits, which reduces taxes. When an employer pays an employee a salary, this amount is an *employee expense*. When an employer contributes to an employee's 401k, this contribution is also an *employee expense* that can be *written off* to reduce taxes for the employer. Many accountants falsely understand that an employee's participation in a pre-tax vehicle lowers the employer's FICA tax burden—but it does not. 401k contributions enjoy pretax status from Federal Income Tax and State Tax rates (where state code is applicable), but it does not (or should not) reduce the employees FICA tax rates. Therefore, the employer receives no additional *tax benefit* of contributing to a pre-tax vehicle or a post-tax vehicle.

Only the employee stands to lose anything upfront in switching from a pre-tax vehicle to a post-tax vehicle. This loss, however, is minuscule when compared to the guaranteed gains and other benefits of the Deferred Income Account. For illustration purposes, let's take a $50 contribution from each paycheck by a 45-year old employee. And, to keep the math simple, let's say that the employer is matching this employee's contribution of $50 with $50.

If this employee were in the 20% tax bracket, he would pay $400 in taxes on a $2,000 paycheck, netting $1,600 per paycheck. But, under the pre-tax scenario, the employee's $50 contribution comes out of the $2,000 bringing his net earnings to $1950. In the 20% tax bracket, his taxes on $1950 would be $390. Therefore, he saves $10 per paycheck in taxes, or $20 per month. And, by calculating this tax savings of $20/month over a 20-year period (at the S&P 500 average of 7.6%), he would realize a $11,635.00 pre-tax contribution savings.

To this amount, we add the growth of the $200 monthly contribution, which was deposited into the taxable 401k account ($50 each paycheck by the employee and employer). At the same 7.6% of the S&P 500, and over the same 20-year period, this $200/month will grow to approximately $116,350.82. These two amounts (the contributions and the pre-tax savings) total about $127,985.82. However, the account value in 20 years is $116,350.82, as the *pre-tax savings* does not factor into the future account balance.

This amount ($116,350.82) is now fully taxable, both the contributions and the growth. In the same 20% tax bracket, the account is actually worth $93,080.66 after taxes.

The recessions of the late 80's, 2000, 2001, and that of 2008 would take this $93,081.00 account down to $55,849.00, thereby requiring a rebounding period of nearly 20 years to arrive back at par.

Also, if you are in these tax-deferred (*qualified*) accounts during your retirement years and during a recession, all the money that you are pulling out of the account to pay for your living expenses will not participate in the rebound. To play it safe, I would plan on at least two deep recessions during your 30-year retirement.

Hypothetically, your 401k of $116,350.82 is reduced to $93,081 by taxes, and further reduced by a recession to $55,849.00; If during a two-year recession, you pulled out $1,000/month to supplement your social security, you would have pulled out $24,000, leaving you with $31,849 in the account to participate in the rebounding of the stock market. The two recent recessions have provided us with a new financial reality. For those individuals already in retirement, this new reality has literally been life shattering.

Taking the same contribution amounts and applying them to the post-tax Deferred Income Account that also averages the same 7.6%, we arrive at the following results:

Through the DIA approach, we lose the $11,635 tax savings over the 20-year period. Therefore, we only have $40 per paycheck to contribute to the retirement account (rather than $50 per paycheck) totaling $160/month of post-tax contributions (which amount includes the employer's post-tax match). At the same 7.6% average, the non-taxable account grows to $93,081.00.

With this $93,081.66, there are never any taxes to pay, nor do we have to worry about the myriad factors that negatively impact the stock market, and therefore most Qualified accounts. We then have to account for *cost of insurance* associated with this account, which (depending of age and health) could be as little as $200/year or as high as $1,000/year), taking the account down from to $73,081.66. But even with this, there is a nice life insurance policy in place for your beneficiaries, creating yet another side benefit of this approach.

Benefits for the Employers

This section will serve mainly as a recap of the employer benefits that have been mentioned throughout the book.

Upon studying the S&P 500 chart in Chapter 7, one can surmise that if the $100,000 fund in 1997 lost its worth to about $78,000 eleven years later in 2008, yet the Deferred Income Account was worth $181,000 in 2008, then a company can feasibly cut its contributions, and still out-produce the 401k.

> [Side Bar: Keep in mind that in a 20% tax bracket, the 401k value of the $78,000 (in 2008) realistically has a value of $62,400 because of taxes.]

This would be extremely valuable to companies who are considering bringing their employee-retirement contributions to an end in this economy. They can now re-educate their employees on a much more efficient retirement program while cutting the company contributions in half.

For companies who have temporarily suspended retirement contributions, it will be a huge expense to bankroll the re-commencement of the 401k program. As mentioned earlier, with the Deferred Income Account, the company can bring on one individual, one department, or one level of management or seniority level at a time. Moreover, it can contribute whatever amounts to whatever individuals it chooses, as it is no longer under the federal mandate of *what you give to one, you must give to all.*

Included in our employee benefits package (at no cost—at the publication of this book) is the mortgage acceleration service, with the added value of having CPAs, accountants, and financial planners administer this program to your employees on an individual basis, providing each employee with advanced financial planning. In revisiting chapters 2 through 6, you will remember that this service retails for an average of $3,500 per person among the various providers. As an employer, you can offer this service to your employees at no charge. Through this service, the average client can pay off his mortgage in an average of 9 years, simply by changing his daily banking practices. This payoff reduction creates an average of $164,000 in mortgage interest savings, which you (as the employer) will be offering to your employees free of charge in your name, as if you were providing it.

This specific service has four distinct purposes within the employee benefits package:

1) To pay off a mortgage in an average of 1/3rd the time of the traditional mortgage.

2) To eliminate consumer debt (as well as student loans) much more quickly, whether an employee has a mortgage or not.

3) To enable the purchase of a home much more quickly by first removing consumer debt. We have the ability to project how much of a home an individual can feasibly afford, when the home can be paid off, and how much interest will be saved with the AMP.

4) To accurately calculate the funding of the employee's retirement.

Also for the employer, the system is much less cumbersome and requires less accounting than the matching structure of the 401k.

If the employer doesn't wish to participate in any employee benefits at all, yet wants to extend the employees some options, we can work with the employees on an individual basis through this same employee benefits package, also at no charge.

There are no annual fees or set-up costs charged to the employer or the employee. It can be presented to the employees as if the employer is offering these services to the employees as a benefit.

Benefits for the Employees

I cannot emphasize enough the fact that individuals can now count on a retirement that is not subject to government or Wall Street corruption, nor to successful terrorist attacks, factors which have historically proven to be devastating to a 401k, IRA, Roth IRA, SEP, and equally devastating to both public and private pensions.

The distributions from the Deferred Income Account are not claimed anywhere on any IRS tax form. As the taxes are paid up front (from every paycheck—ergo *post-tax*), the IRS is wholly removed from the transactions of this retirement account when the employee adheres to the guidelines. Each employee will have access to our CPA staff throughout his/her lifetime to ensure proper guidance and accurate answers for the more advanced estate planning issues.

The employee receives advanced education on finance that will completely change his/her life. The banking practices of these individuals will change dramatically. If individuals are purchasing and paying off homes in an average of 9 years, saving an average of $164,000 in mortgage interest, they can then take a more active and aggressive role in funding their own retirement, putting them decades ahead in the retirement realm.

Also with this financial education come more advanced concepts, such as better health insurance strategies, or how to purchase/finance large ticket items more efficiently, enabling the employees to *become their own bank*. Again, all at no charge to the employees participating in the employee benefits package.

When an employee changes employment, the Deferred Income Account and the Hybrid-Health Insurance Program are fully portable, rendering COBRA, and the accounting and tracing of (and compliance to) COBRA requirement completely irrelevant.

Our CPA staff continues the administration of the individual's employee benefits. The employee will have the assistance of our CPA staff for any advice and/or assistance in approaching the new employer, and in setting up or negotiating contributions to his/her account (rather than having the new employer set up a 401k for that individual).

Individuals Facing Employer Obstacles

If you would like to participate in this employee benefits package, but you feel your employer is standing in your way, either I or my staff would be more than happy to meet with you and show you how we can provide these same benefits to you personally, enabling you to opt out of your employer's benefits program completely.

Our benefits package will outdo anything your employer can currently offer you. If your employer is currently contributing $200/month to your retirement, how many years will it take until his $200 contribution equals $164,000? [The average amount saved in reconfiguring your financial practices.] Answer: 68 years. Now, if a portion of that $164,000 savings is able to then be directed into a non-taxable, no-market-loss account for your retirement, you will be hard pressed to find any vehicle on the planet that comes close to this productivity.

Self-Employed, Network Marketers, and Direct Marketers

Having lived the last 30 years of my life in Utah (during the notable rise of the local network-marketing behemoths such as NuSkin, Nature's Sunshine, Synergy, Usana, Young Living, Tahitian Noni, Xocai, Xango, Neways, Nature's Way, *et al*; and, having sat through and presented many of my concepts to their audiences, I feel I can knowledgably and confidently state the following:

> *While most of these companies offer great opportunities, one common downside is "the bridge of tears": The point at which an individual decides to quit his/her job and become truly self-employed.*

On this *bridge of tears*, not only is regular and reliable income drastically reduced, but also group-health and retirement benefits are normally eliminated—thereby creating either an enormous risk (should these individuals decide not to replace their health insurance), or a tremendous burden on their budgets (if these individuals opt to secure their own health coverage). It took me 8 years of self-employment before I discovered that the bridge of tears disappears under this three-phase employee benefits system: Debt & Mortgage acceleration, tax-free/no-market loss retirement, and the affordable Hybrid Health Insurance approach based on individual risk assessment. These three foundational buttresses provide one with peace of mind while getting across that bridge.

Mortgage/Debt Acceleration (based on the Australian banking practices): As explained in the first six chapters, by changing your daily banking and financial behaviors, you can save 2/3rd of your interest payable. In terms of a mortgage, the average client savings in mortgage interest is about $164,000. This is substantial savings in getting you across that bridge. However, in reality, a decrease in income (by quitting your job) may not allow you to accelerate your mortgage, so we look at this on a case-by-case basis. The buffer account concept however delivers tremendous peace of mind.

Healthcare for Individuals: For the details of this aspect, you will want to read Chapter 8 in its entirety. In the overall plan (and depending on your budget), you can obtain substantial coverage for as little as $28/month for an individual, and $40/month for a family.

In a one particular case, a self-employed client was rejected by her insurance carrier because of cancer. Her CT scans cost her $2,000 per visit, and she required 2 visits per year. However, on the $28/month Core-plan, her network costs were reduced to $400/visit, saving her $3,200 per year. There are a plethora of stories of this type wherein an eclectically creative healthcare approach can cut insurance costs in half for both employers and individuals alike.

In another scenario, our staff fought for a self-employed cancer patient over a 7-month period. Being a cancer survivor for more than 5 years, her family health insurance costs were $2,000/month. At the end of our process, her premiums were reduced to $680/month for her family, saving $1,320/month.

> [Side Bar: The travesty of our broken healthcare system is that it is stripping America of its entrepreneurial spirit, drive, and creativity for this single reason: Because individual healthcare plans and medical costs are so unbearably expensive, if something happens to an entrepreneur in the start-up years of his/her business, these entrepreneurs are forced to put their efforts on hold (or abandon them completely), having to return to the corporate workforce attaching widget A to widget B on an assembly line simply to obtain affordable *group coverage*. This is a sad reality in the current U.S. healthcare system and the state of entrepreneurs of America.
>
> Again, speaking as a fiscal conservative, the political right has done nothing to remedy this stripping America of its entrepreneurs. What is more sobering about the right-wing ideology of healthcare (in terms of non-regulation) is this: As an entrepreneur (since leaving a Fortune 500 Company's in 1996), I have paid for health insurance. If, however, at any time I or my family contract some major illness, under the pre-Obamacare healthcare structure the insurance company could rate me up to where I would be forced from their rolls. Let me state that again for emphasis: I have paid for insurance premiums for 30 years, yet by contracting an illness, that insurance company (who has received 30 years of my premiums) can reject me in a matter of months (on January 1 of the following year when the new insurance-year starts). This is a worthless system, and one can hardly fault the left wing for attempting to rectify these fiscal injustices. If the political right doesn't like

socialized medicine, then they should have provided solutions first—before the left did!

That said, I am certainly not endorsing Obamacare or socialized medicine, as we simply cannot afford it given the current state of the economy (coupled with America's grotesquely unhealthy behaviors); BUT, at least it will serve as an undergirding to America's greatest resource: its entrepreneurial spirit and innovation. Perhaps an entrepreneur spared from having to return to the corporate assembly line (simply for insurance coverage) can come up with a way of how America *can* afford it...

Note: The financial concepts in this book can save the average American household over $300,000 over a ten-year period. This alone could wipe out the National Debt: $53,000 per capita (as of 2012) X 2.48 people per household = $131,440/household). But don't tell Washington this: they'll wipe this savings out too!]

The options we can provide in the healthcare arena create substantial savings, inside or outside of the parameters of Obamacare if providers continue to provide the products.

Retirement Account Transitioning: Once an individual ventures into the self-employment arena, he/she also forfeits his/her *employer-matching* retirement contributions. This is the prime opportunity to transition your retirement into something much more stable and reliable without any further market loss or taxes.

For the self-employed or for employees whose employers cannot afford employee benefits, there are many affordable options available to you.

Chapter 10: Conclusion

Throughout decades of government evolution in the *modern* western world, it is self-evident that these governments have failed to provide a sense of security to the masses, be it financial security in retirement or physical security in the wake of natural disasters. The systems and structures, as currently constituted, have either failed or are projected to fail. This is not news.

Therefore, in regards to

- **the national and individual debt crisis:** There is no safe harbor, only self-reliance through the tenets of redistributive modeling.

- **the national retirement crisis:** The only silver lining for retirement (thus far) is based on self-reliance and self-motivation to become educated on other investment options: Redistributive modeling is a great starting point.

- **the national disease epidemics:** There is no magic pill, only self-nutrition to enhance self-preservation. In these redistributive models, your physical health will directly affect your financial health. For the vast majority of the masses, there is no way around this.

- **the national healthcare crisis:** There is no economical systemic fix, only self-determination to reduce your risks (as best you can) while limiting your dependence and reliance on the overly-inflated and broken system.

It all comes down to the individual; to the ONE. Personal responsibility will cushion you and soften the blows from the looming crises. Only when enough individuals take upon them*selves* the responsibility to solve these issues for them*selves* will the country will begin to heal economically and politically—despite government policy.

Redistributive Modeling provides the most effective methods of elevating the masses to the financial position where they can become more independent of these failing systems, and less dependent on government (be it through subsidies, grants, bailouts, handouts, etc.), while simultaneously enabling individuals to productively contribute to society as well as to the economy.

Its policies neither favor the political left or right, but are simply geared to bringing about productive solutions and immediate results for the household through consumer-driven systemic changes—*Redistributive Modeling.*

Ronald Karren
American Financial Planner, Inc.
P.O. Box 1286
Pleasant Grove, UT 84062
800-614-1550